FLORAL NEEDLEPOINT
FOR BEGINNERS

FLORAL NEEDLEPOINT FOR BEGINNERS

DECORATIVE DESIGNS FOR
SPRING, SUMMER, FALL & WINTER

STELLA EDWARDS

NEW
BURLINGTON
BOOKS

A QUINTET BOOK

Published by New Burlington Books
6 Blundell Street
London N7 9BH

ISBN 1-85348-620-5

This book was designed and produced by
Quintet Publishing Limited
6 Blundell Street
London N7 9BH

Creative Director: Richard Dewing
Designer: James Lawrence
Project Editor: Helen Denholm
Editor: Lydia Darbyshire
Photographers: Martin Norris and
Nelson Hargreaves

Typeset in Great Britain by
Central Southern Typesetters, Eastbourne
Manufactured in Hong Kong by
Regent Publishing Services Limited
Printed in Singapore by Star Standard Industries Pte. Ltd.

CONTENTS

INTRODUCTION **6**

MATERIALS **8**

TECHNIQUES **11**

INTRODUCTION

NEEDLEPOINT is a most rewarding pastime. Not only is there the pleasure that comes from time spent making something beautiful, but there is also the satisfaction of seeing the finished article, which may be admired and used for many years to come.

Needlepoint began to be popular about two hundred years ago, when ladies embroidered designs they had copied from woven tapestries onto canvas fabric. This practice has led to a certain amount of confusion between the words "needlepoint" and "tapestry". Needlepoint is a form of embroidery in which stitches are used to cover an open canvas; tapestry, on the other hand, is a fabric that is woven on a jacquard loom.

In recent years needlepoint has enjoyed a huge revival in popularity, and there is a wide and ever-increasing range of designs and projects to make, ranging from kits that come complete with the necessary yarns, to pre-printed canvases, to plain canvases in a variety of mesh sizes on which you can work patterns and designs of your own choice. The selection of colours in both tapestry wools and stranded cottons is tremendous, and by mixing colours and textures you can create all manner of designs and patterns.

In this book I have concentrated on small, straight-forward projects in the hope that once you have mastered the basic stitches and techniques you will be inspired and confident enough to tackle some much larger and grander pieces.

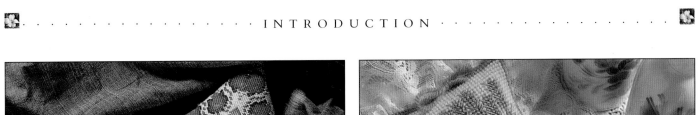

MATERIALS

YARNS

Anchor yarns have been used to work all the projects in this book and the numbers on the colour charts refer to Anchor yarns. You can, of course, substitute these for any make of needlepoint yarns you wish to use and match the colours accordingly. Tapisserie wool and stranded cotton are available in a wide range of colours from needlework or haberdashery shops and from the haberdashery departments of most large department stores.

When I used stranded cotton to work the designs, I used all six strands together. If you are working in cross stitch on an evenweave fabric such as Aida, you will usually divide the strands to work more delicate stitches. When I am working with stranded cotton on canvas, however, I find that all six strands are needed to cover the canvas completely.

You can use different colours of tapisserie wool and stranded cotton from those used for the projects illustrated here. You may, for example, want to make a picture or cushion cover to coordinate with the colour scheme in a particular room or to make some matching accessories for a favourite bag. Remember that the tones of all the colours you use should be similar. If you decided to re-work in pastel shades the Pansy Tissue Box Cover, for which I had selected very strong colours, you should change all the colours to pastel tones, or the design will look unbalanced.

You will also need ordinary cotton sewing thread to complete some of the projects.

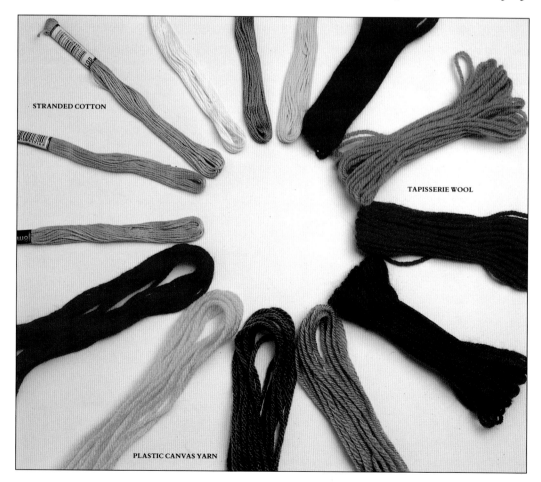

LEFT *Here are the three main types of cotton and yarn used in the projects in this book. You will be able to purchase a wide range of colours in each.*

OPPOSITE *These are the six types of canvas used in the needlepoint projects in this book.*

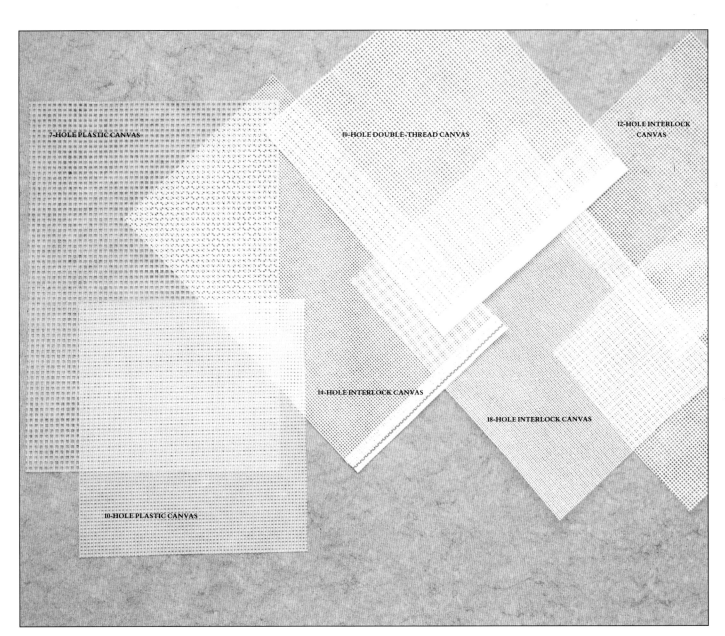

CANVAS

Canvas is available in several different sizes, ranging from 5 to 24 holes to 1 inch (2.5 cm). Most of the projects illustrated in this book were worked on 10- or 12-hole canvas – that is, there are 10 or 12 holes or threads to 1 inch (2.5 cm) – although I occasionally used 14- and 18-hole canvas when I was using the finer, stranded cotton yarns.

Many of the designs in this book can be adapted to make alternative articles. One of the simplest and most effective ways of adapting a design is to change the number of holes per inch (2.5 cm) on the fabric on which you are working so that the design becomes larger or smaller. If, for example, you wanted to use the design for the Poppy Gift Tag to make a picture, you could work it on 12-hole canvas with wool instead of the 18-hole canvas and stranded cottons that were used to make the gift tag. Following the chart will give you a picture almost double the size of the gift tag.

Similarly, if you want to make a particular design smaller, use a canvas with more holes to the inch (2.5 cm) – for example, you could use an 18-hole canvas instead of a 10-hole canvas.

Most of the designs in this book can be adapted in this way, so that you can make a pincushion to match the needlecases or a matching purse, spectacles case and key ring fob. Remember that when you adapt a design, especially if you are making it larger, you will have to adjust the quantities of wool or stranded cotton that you buy.

NEEDLES

The yarn you use will vary according to the mesh of canvas you choose, and, obviously, the larger the mesh, the thicker the yarn you will need. This, in turn, means that you will need a larger size of needle. Tapestry needles are widely available. They are round- or blunt-ended and are designed to pass through the holes of your canvas without snagging or catching on the neighbouring stitches, which can distort your design. Tapestry needles are available in sizes from 13 to 26, but I have tended to use the standard size 20 for most of the designs. When I have used the thicker plastic yarn canvas I have used a size 18 needle, and when I have used stranded cotton I used a size 22 needle.

You will also need some ordinary sharp sewing needles for attaching linings and so forth.

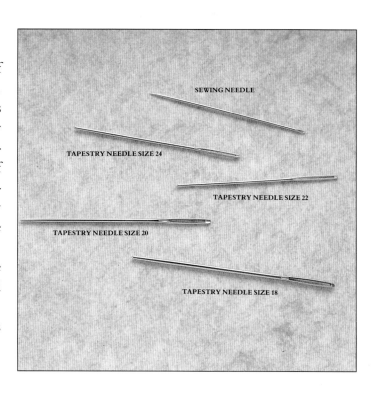

LINING FABRIC

To make up most of the projects you will need some pretty cotton fabric for lining or backing your work. Any odd pieces you have left over from dressmaking can be used, and you might want to try putting several coordinating colours together to achieve a particularly striking effect.

FILLING

I have used polyester toy stuffing, which is available from most haberdashers and craft shops, to fill pincushions and herb sachets. However, there are many kinds of filling to choose from. Some people recommend that sheep's wool should be used in pincushions because the natural oil in the wool keeps the needles clean and sharp. Other people like to use sawdust, while others use cut-up pieces of stockings or tights.

FINISHING TOUCHES

The addition of ribbons and bows will give a professional finish to your projects, and beads and metallic threads can be used to give sparkle. I have used these on several projects, and they are included in the appropriate lists of materials, but you could add them to any of the projects to make them even more personal and special.

ABOVE To complete the projects in this book you will need a basic selection of needles, as shown here.

TECHNIQUES

STARTING AND FINISHING

When you begin to work with a new colour of yarn, do not tie a knot in the end. Instead, leave an end about 1 in (2.5 cm) long and catch it down as you stitch so that it cannot work loose. When you are finishing off, slip the needle carefully through the back of a few stitches and cut off the end neatly. This will give a smooth, flat surface on the right side.

I find that working with lengths of 15 in (38 cm) is best. If the yarn is any longer than this it tends to fray as it is continually drawn through the canvas, and it may then break, which can be a nuisance, or it becomes thin, which will result in uneven-looking stitches.

If you find that the edge of the canvas catches against the yarn you are using or against your clothes as you work, cover the raw edges with masking tape.

Finally, always remember to work in good light. If you find you are having problems distinguishing colours, you are straining your eyes. Colours can look different under artificial light. Special light bulbs that simulate daylight are now available, and if you do a lot of needle-work in the evening it is worth obtaining one of these. Alternatively, use a high-watt bulb in a spot light or an angle-poise lamp, so that the light is directed onto your work.

MARKING CANVAS

Some people find it helpful to mark the centre of the canvas before they begin. If you do this, always use a waterproof pen. A non-waterproof marker could run when you dampen the work for blocking and ruin it.

TENSION

It is important to keep the tension of the stitches the same throughout your work or you will get a bumpy, uneven finish. Practise working a few stitches with wool or cotton to see what comes naturally. If you have a tendency to pull the stitches too tightly, the holes in the canvas will appear between your stitches and the canvas itself may even begin to curl. If you stitch loosely, there is a danger that stitches may snag on sharp points and corners and your work will be spoiled. Don't despair if you do have problems achieving an even tension – a good pressing with a hot steam iron over a damp cloth will work wonders!

STRETCHING AND PRESSING

In the instructions for all the projects I have mentioned that the work has to be stretched and pressed, a process known as blocking. This is because, no matter how carefully you work and no matter how even your stitches are, your embroidery will tend to go out of skew as you stitch and will need to be straightened to give a professional look to the finished article.

Embroidery frames are available and can help to keep your work straight by keeping the canvas threads in alignment. However, most of the projects are so small that it may be difficult to fasten the canvas into the frame. If you do have a slate or scroll frame you can securely attach the edges of your piece of canvas to strips of strong, firm material, which you can then fasten to the webbing on the horizontal rollers and, if necessary, lace to the vertical pieces.

However, even if you have used a frame, you will improve the appearance of your work if you stretch and press it. When you have finished a design, gently and evenly dampen the embroidery with water and pin it, face down, on a covered board. Use rust-proof drawing pins and place them quite close together, making sure that you exert even tension in all directions and that the edges are perfectly square. A set square (triangle) is useful for making sure that the horizontal and vertical threads are perfectly aligned and that the corners are square. Leave your work to dry, which can take several hours or even overnight. When it is completely dry, remove the pins and press it with a hot steam iron over a damp cloth. The embroidery should then be ready to make up into the project.

If, after sewing together two pieces of embroidery – the two sides of a pincushion or spectacles case, for example – you find that the work will not lie flat, try pressing the work, again using a hot steam iron over a damp cloth, and leaving it to dry for a couple of hours under a heavy weight such as a pile of books.

C U T T I N G   C O R N E R S

When you have finished stitching the design for a cushion or pincushion or for an article that is to be lined, the corners of the canvas will need to be cut so that the turned-in edges lie neatly and are not too bulky. Take great care not to cut either the hole in which the first stitch is formed or the yarn itself.

F R A M I N G

Many of the designs in this book could be made into pictures by mounting them on a board and framing them.

When you have finished the embroidery and have blocked your work so that it is perfectly square, cut a piece of board, which should be about ¼ in (6 mm) thick and slightly smaller both horizontally and vertically than the finished work. Use pins to hold the stitched canvas to the board, pushing the pins into the edge of the board and stretching the canvas as tightly and evenly as you can. You may have to replace and repin as you work around the edge, and you must make sure that the threads of the canvas are perfectly square and true. Use a large herringbone stitch to lace the sides of the canvas together, working first vertically and then horizontally, and beginning in the centre and working outwards to the corners.

L O O K I N G   A F T E R   Y O U R   W O R K

Because needlepoint is worked in pure wool or cotton yarn and is stitched on cotton canvas, it will last for years and years. In stately homes all over Britain there are examples of needlepoint chair seat covers that are several hundreds of years old.

Needlepoint can, however, get dirty, and perhaps the best way to clean it is to rub it gently with a proprietary dry cleaning solvent. Several excellent "spot" dry cleaning preparations specially designed for cleaning upholstery are available.

Alternatively, if a stain proves impossible to remove, you could carefully unpick the area and re-stitch it. Be very careful not to tug at the stitches when you pull them out; gently and cautiously snip at the yarn with a pair of sharp scissors. Then carefully re-stitch the area, lightly pressing it under a damp cloth when you have finished it. It is probably a good idea to keep some lengths of yarn when you have finished a project so that if you do need to re-stitch an area in the future, matching the colours will not be a problem.

S T I T C H E S

Most of the designs are worked in half cross stitch, which is easy and quick to do. I have occasionally introduced cross stitch if a design needs to look square – for example, cross stitch is used for the letters in the Busy Lizzie Calendar. Cross stitch has the effect of blocking the stitch, compared with half cross stitch, which runs diagonally. In two of the designs – the Christmas Tree Decoration and Snowman Card – I have used French knots, which are easy to do and give a neat, raised stitch. You could add them to other designs if you wished. Also in the Snowman Card I have used chain stitch for the details of the leaves. Again, this is easy to work and looks effective.

—— HALF CROSS STITCH ——

You can work this stitch from right to left or from left to right. Bring your needle through to the front of your work and insert it into the next diagonal hole down to the left or right. Then bring your needle to the front through the hole vertically above the hole you have just taken your yarn through. Repeat until you have worked across the row, then repeat the procedure on the next row. On the right side of your work, all the diagonal stitches will slant in the same direction; on the back of your work you will see rows of short, vertical stitches.

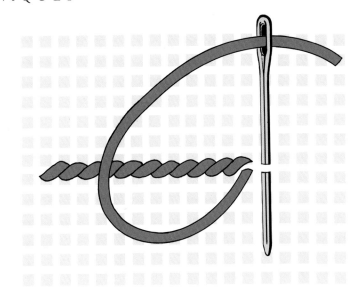

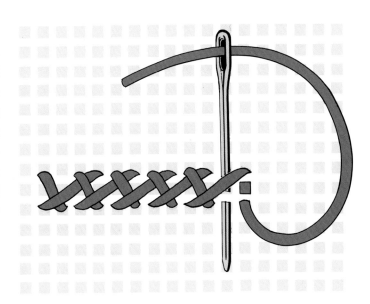

—— CROSS STITCH ——

There are two ways of working cross stitch. Both methods produce neat rows of vertical stitches on the wrong side of your work.

If you are covering a fairly large area in a single colour, work in horizontal rows. First, working from right to left, complete one row of evenly spaced diagonal stitches, as if you were working a row of half cross stitch. Then, working from left to right, complete the stitches by adding the diagonal cross.

If you are working a few isolated stitches or a diagonal row, complete each cross stitch before moving on to the next one.

Remember: the most important feature of cross stitch is that all the top stitches must slant in the same direction.

—— LONG-ARMED CROSS STITCH ——

This decorative stitch, which is sometimes also called long-legged cross stitch, is used to join the fronts and back of items such as pincushions. It is worked in much the same way as basic cross stitch, but each stitch is completed before the next one is begun. Make the first diagonal stitch upwards from left to right before completing the second, top stitch. The first stitch should be twice as long as the second stitch. This stitch is worked two holes forward and one hole back so it completely covers the canvas.

FRENCH KNOTS

These stitches can be worked very easily, and, with a little practice, you will be able to create groups of evenly shaped knots.

Bring your yarn through to the right side of your work and hold it down with your thumb. Wind the yarn around the needle, and pull the needle through. Insert the needle in the canvas just behind the point at which you brought it through to form a neat knot.

Alternatively, bring your needle through to the right side of your work but do not pull it right through. Wind the yarn around the needle once or twice, depending on how large you want the knot to be, and draw the needle through the knot, holding the yarn close to the surface of your work with your thumb. Stitch back into the canvas near to the starting point, pulling the knot tight. Repeat as often as required.

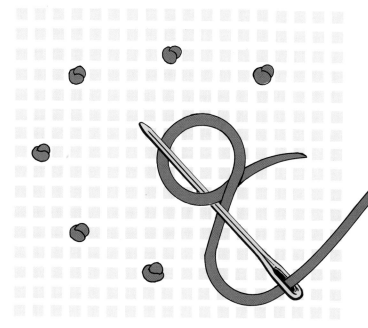

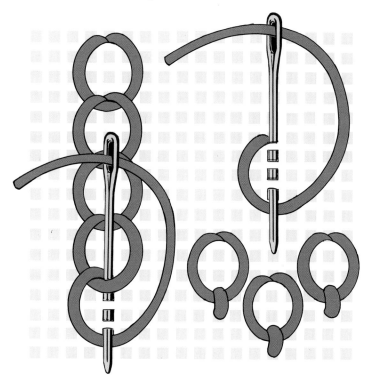

CHAIN STITCH

You will probably find it easiest to work downwards. Bring the yarn through to the right side and stitch back into the same point, holding the loop of thread so created with the thumb of your left hand (if you are left-handed, hold the loop with the thumb of your right hand). Bring the point of your needle up a short distance from your first stitch and into the centre of the loop, pulling up the slack yarn but making sure that you do not pull it so tightly that you spoil the chain-like appearance of the row of stitches. Stitch back each time into the exit point of the stitch you have just made.

For detached chain stitches, when the needle has been brought up through the loop of the working yarn to complete the stitch, take it down again over one horizontal thread of the canvas into the hole immediately below. In this way it ties the loop down.

SLIP STITCH

This is a neat way of joining your embroidered canvas to the lining fabric so that no unworked canvas can be seen. Working from right to left, bring your needle through the folded edge of the fabric. Pick up a thread of the opposite fabric, then slip the needle through the folded edge for about ⅛ in (3 mm) before bringing it through to make the next stitch. When it is worked correctly, slip stitch is almost invisible.

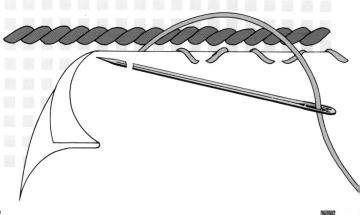

SPRING

DAFFODIL NEEDLECASE

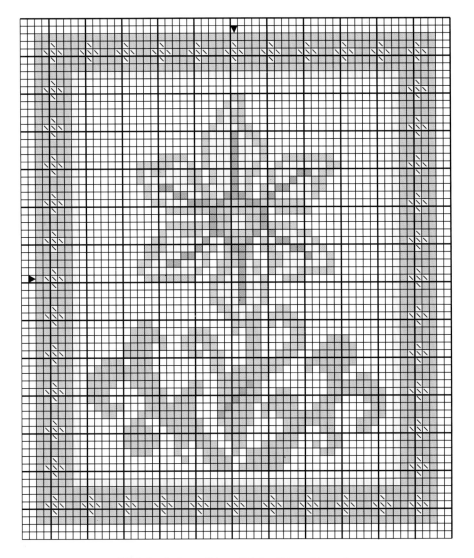

Finished size: 4½ × 5½ in (11 × 14 cm)

A NEEDLECASE IS AN ABSOLUTE MUST FOR KEEPING
SAFE ALL THOSE NEEDLES THAT SOMEHOW ALWAYS
SEEM TO DISAPPEAR WHEN THEY ARE MOST NEEDED.
THE DAFFODIL DESIGN CAN BE EASILY ADAPTED TO
CREATE A COORDINATING PINCUSHION, OR IF YOU
WISH YOU CAN USE IT TO MAKE A COVER FOR A
NOTEBOOK.

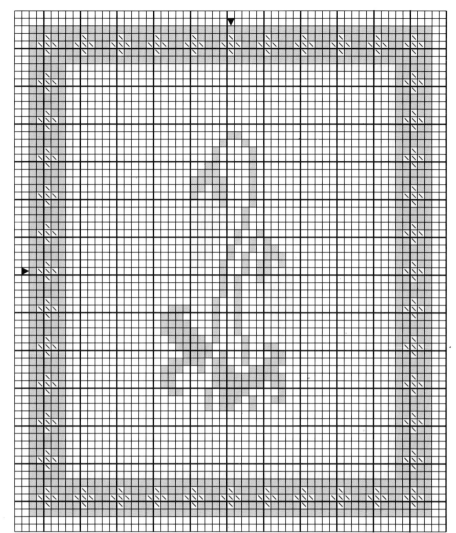

1 Follow the chart to work the design, starting in the middle (indicated by the arrows on the edges). Begin stitching with the biscuit-coloured wool to form the outline of the daffodil. The colours on the charts and in the key correspond with wool colours and numbers.

2 Fill in the shape using the bright yellow wool; then add the darker orange detail. Then stitch the green leaves.

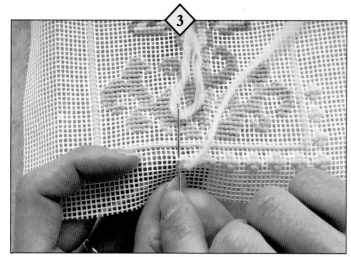

3 Stitch the border, using cross stitch to make the motifs square. Make sure that the top stitch of each cross lies in the opposite direction to the rest of the work.

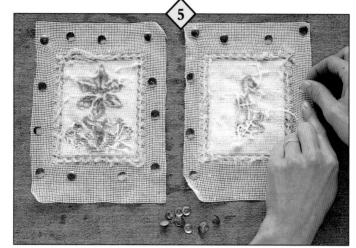

4 The finished front and back before stretching.

5 Dampen the embroidery with water and pin it face down on a board covered with a clean cloth to straighten the embroidery. When the embroidery is dry, unpin it and press it with a hot steam iron over a damp cloth.

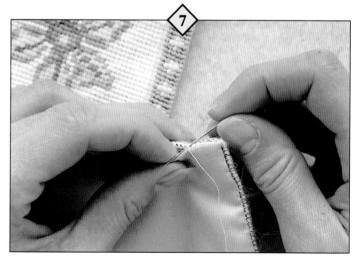

6 Trim the canvas, cutting the corners at an angle.

7 Line the back of each piece, making sure the edges of the canvas are turned in neatly.

8 *Stitch the front and back together using long-armed cross stitch. The white wool has been used here, but you could use yellow or green if you wanted.*

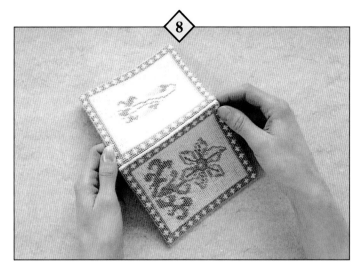

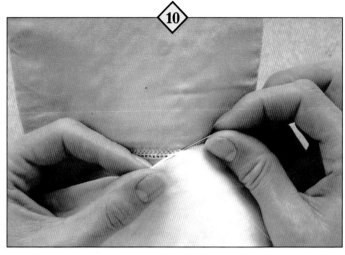

9 *Fold a piece of felt and cut it to size so that it is slightly smaller than the size of the needlecase. Use pinking shears to give a zigzag edge.*

10 *Carefully sew the felt to the inside seam of the needlecase. Press with a steam iron over a damp cloth to finish.*

BLUEBELL CREDIT CARD HOLDER

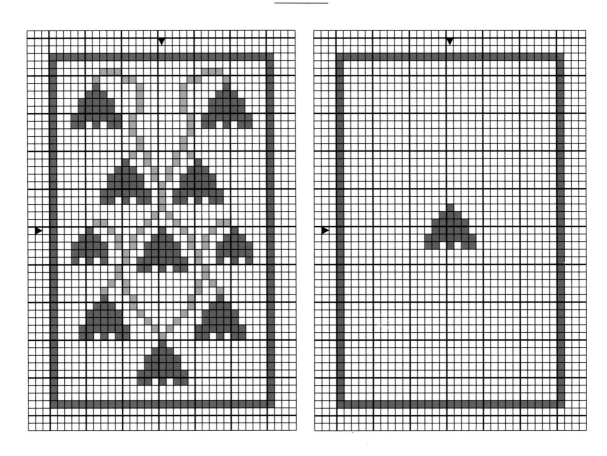

Finished size: 3 × 3¾ in (7.5 × 9.5 cm)

KEY	
☐	8012
▦	9100
▧	8690

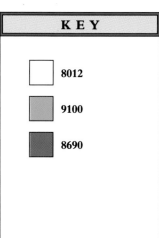

THIS PRETTY HOLDER CAN BE USED FOR ALL SORTS OF CREDIT CARDS. I HAVE ATTACHED ONLY ONE POCKET TO THE INSIDE, BUT IT WOULD BE EASY ENOUGH TO SEW ANOTHER TO THE OPPOSITE SIDE. IF YOU WANT IT TO HOLD MORE CARDS, ADD EXTRA POCKETS MADE FROM THE LINING FABRIC AND ATTACH THEM TO THE CENTRAL SEAM.

MATERIALS

- Tapestry wool: 1 skein of 8690; 2 skeins of 8012; short length of 9100
- 2 pieces of 12-hole interlock canvas, each 5 × 6 in (12.5 × 15 cm)
- 1 piece of lining fabric 4 × 5 in (10 × 12.5cm)

1 Follow the chart to work the design, starting in the middle (indicated by the arrows on the edges). Use half cross stitch throughout. The colours on the charts and in the key correspond with the wool colours and numbers.

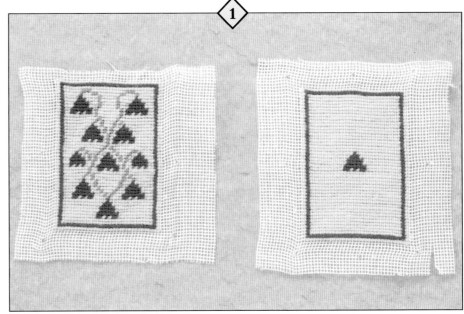

2 After stretching the embroidery, press it with a hot steam iron over a damp cloth and then trim back the canvas, cutting the corners at an angle.

3 Cut a piece of lining fabric slightly larger than the embroidery and sew it to the wrong sides, turning in the edges to give a neat finish.

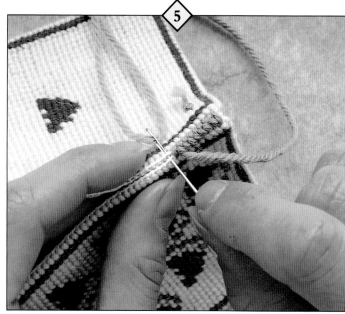

4 Sew another, smaller piece of lining fabric to one side to make a pocket. Make sure that the edges are neatly finished.

5 Stitch together the front and back, wrong sides together, using long-armed cross stitch. Press the finished credit card holder with a hot steam iron over a damp cloth and it will be ready for use.

PANSY TISSUE
BOX COVER

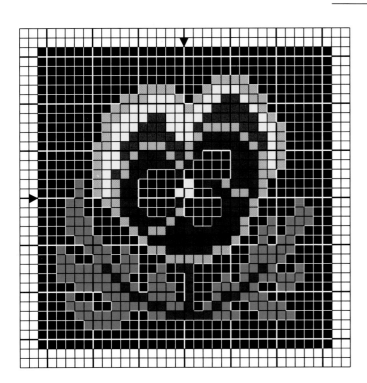
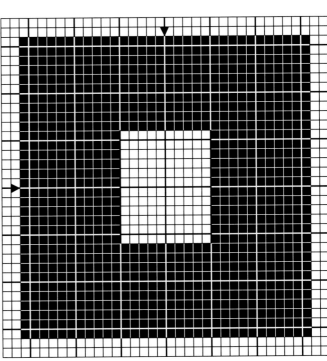

<table>
<tr><td colspan="2">KEY</td></tr>
</table>

	230
	245
	901
	917
	676
	686
	12

Finished size: 5⅛ × 5⅛ × 5⅛ in (13.5 × 13.5 × 13.5 cm)

THIS COLOURFUL BOX HAS BEEN MADE FROM PLASTIC CANVAS, WHICH IS AS EASY TO WORK AS THE COTTON CANVAS BUT HAS A STIFFNESS THAT IS USEFUL FOR THREE-DIMENSIONAL STRUCTURES.

MATERIALS

- Plastic canvas yarn: 1 skein each of 245, 917, 901, 230 and 686; 3 skeins of 676; 5 skeins of 12
- One sheet of 7-hole, clear plastic canvas, 21 × 13 in (53.5 × 33 cm)

1 Follow the chart to work the design, starting in the middle (indicated by the arrows on the edges). Use half cross stitch throughout. The colours on the charts and in the key correspond with the yarn colours and numbers. Stitch four of these, one for each side.

2 Stitch the top in black wool only, following the chart.

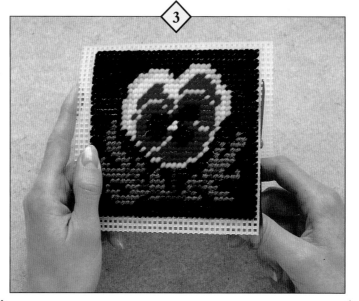

3 Trim back the canvas on each side panel and the top. There is no need to block plastic canvas.

4 Carefully cut out the hole in the top piece of canvas. Then overstitch the edge with black wool.

5 Stitch the sides together using a long-armed cross stitch. I have used contrasting green wool, but you could use any other colour you liked.

6 · Stitch the top to the sides, again using a long-armed cross stitch.

7 · Oversew the bottom edge with black wool.

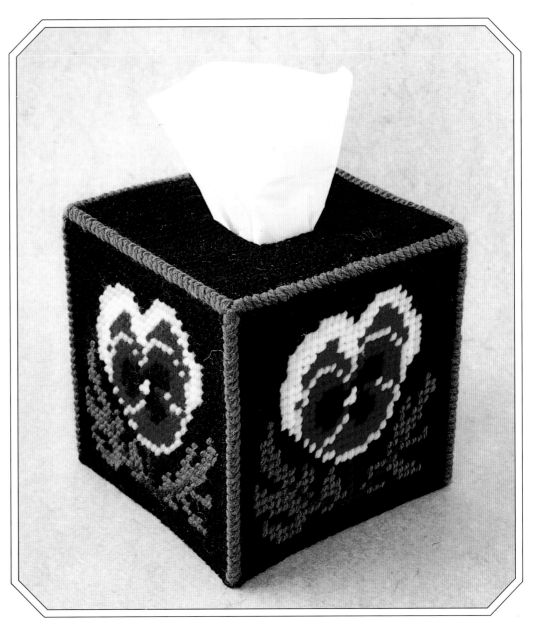

PRIMROSE PICTURE

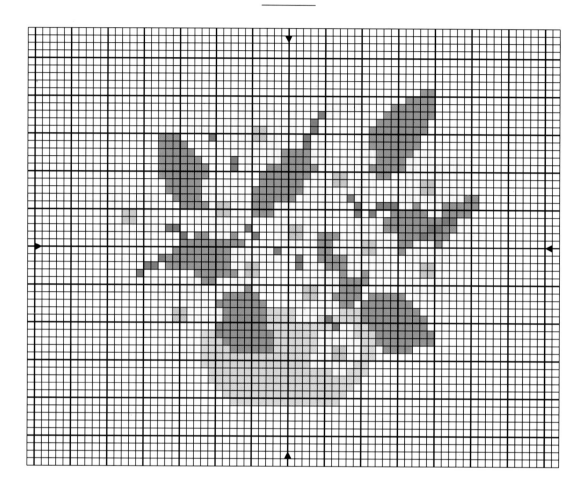

KEY

☐	1
☐	292
▨	74
▨	291
▨	225
▨	227

Finished size: 4¾ × 3¾ in (12 × 9.5 cm)

THIS DELICATE PICTURE OF FRESH PRIMROSES WILL BRIGHTEN ANY WALL AND BE A REMINDER OF SPRING SUNSHINE ALL YEAR ROUND. IT IS STITCHED WITH STRANDED COTTONS, WHICH GIVE A LUSTROUS SHEEN, AND IT IS QUICK AND EASY TO MAKE.

MATERIALS

- Stranded cotton: 1 skein each of 292 and 225; 2 skeins of 1; short lengths of 291, 74 and 227
- 1 piece of 14-hole interlock canvas, 7 × 6 in (17.5 × 15 cm)
- Card mount
- Adhesive tape
- Paper to back

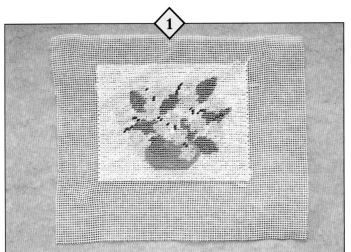

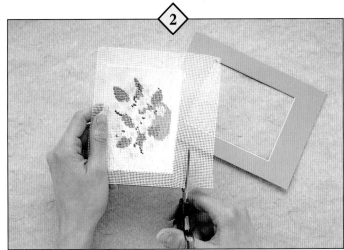

1 *Follow the chart to work the design, starting in the middle (indicated by the arrows on the edges). Use half cross stitch throughout. The colours on the chart and in the key correspond with the stranded cotton colours and numbers.*

2 *After stretching the embroidery, press it with a hot steam iron. Trim back the canvas and make sure that the edge of the canvas does not show when the card mount is placed over it. Position the card mount over the embroidery, using adhesive tape at the back to hold it in place.*

3 *Back the picture with a piece of thick, white paper or card to hide the ends. Once the picture has been mounted in this way it can then be framed by a professional framer if you wish.*

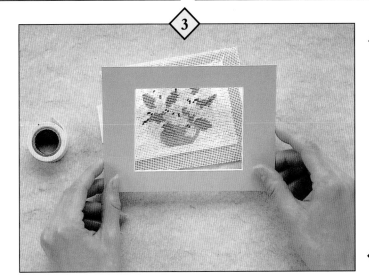

CROCUS
PENCIL CASE

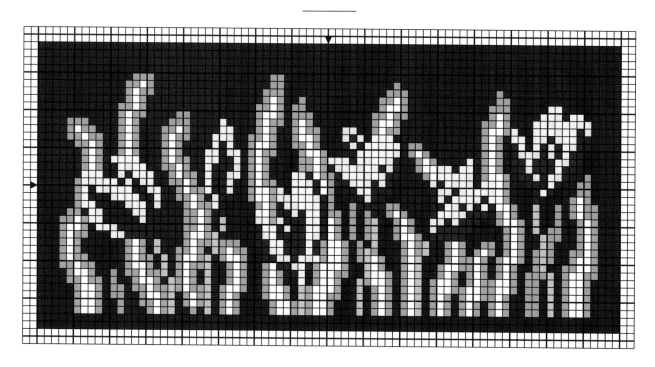

KEY

☐	8006
☐	8036
☐	8112
▨	9096
▨	9100
■	9640
■	8612

Finished size: 7¾ × 3¾ in (20 × 9.5 cm)

THIS DESIGN COULD ALSO BE STITCHED AND USED AS A MAKE-UP BAG OR A PURSE. YOU COULD EVEN ADD SOME BEADS AND OVERSTITCH IN GOLD THREADS TO MAKE A DELIGHTFUL EVENING BAG.

MATERIALS

- Tapestry wool: 1 skein each of 8612, 8036 and 8006; 2 skeins of 9100; 3 skeins of 9640; short lengths of 9096 and 8112
- 2 pieces of 10-hole, double-thread canvas, each 10 × 6 in (25 × 15 cm)
- 2 pieces of lining fabric, each 8½ × 4½ in (22 × 11 cm)
- Velcro

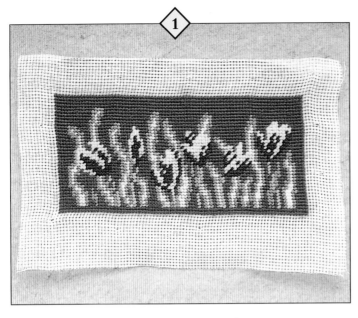

1 Follow the chart to work the design, starting in the middle (indicated by the arrows on the edges). Use half cross stitch throughout. The colours on the chart and in the key correspond with the wool colours and numbers. Work two pieces, one for the front and one for the back.

2 After stretching the embroidery, press it with a hot steam iron over a damp cloth. Trim back the canvas, cutting the corners at an angle.

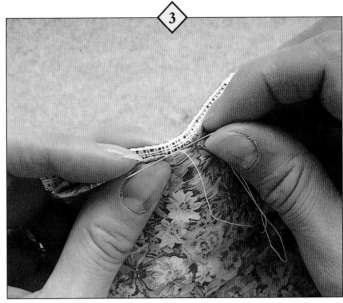

3 Sew a piece of pretty lining fabric to each side, making sure that no lining shows over the top edge of the embroidery.

4 Sew a piece of Velcro along the top of each side.

5 *Stitch the front and back together with long-armed cross stitch. If any canvas peeps through at the corners, overstitch it with the purple wool to cover.*

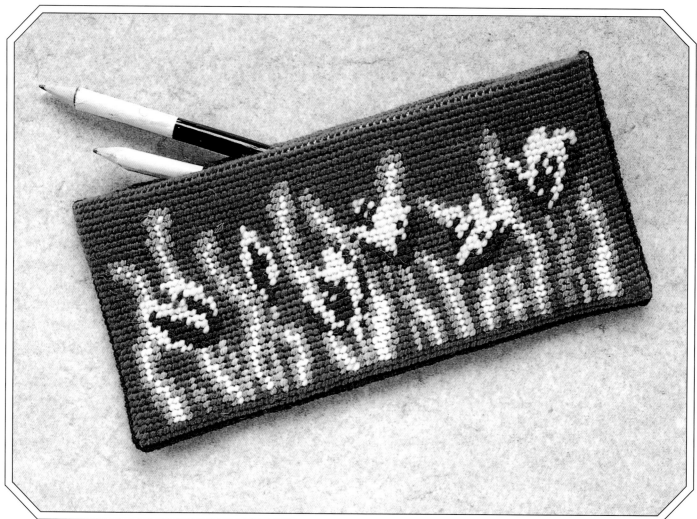

CHERRY BLOSSOM CARD

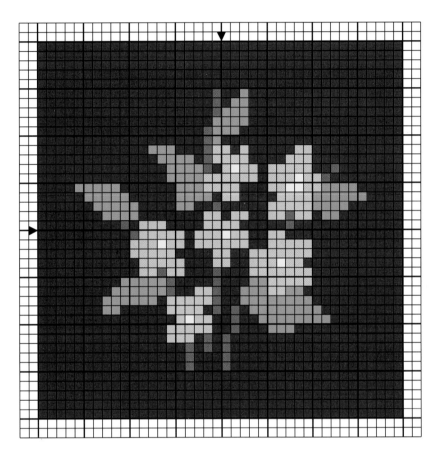

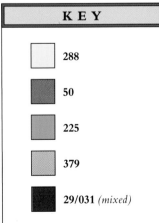

KEY	
	288
	50
	225
	379
	29/031 *(mixed)*

Finished size: 3 in (7.5 cm) across

THIS BRIGHT, CHEERFUL CARD COULD BE USED FOR A BIRTHDAY OR AS A SPECIAL VALENTINE'S DAY CARD. ADDING FINE METALLIC THREAD TO THE STRANDED COTTON AS YOU STITCH MAKES THE BACKGROUND SHIMMER WHEN IT CATCHES THE LIGHT. GREETINGS CARDS FOR MOUNTING EMBROIDERY ARE AVAILABLE FROM NEEDLECRAFT AND HABERDASHERY SHOPS.

MATERIALS

- Stranded cotton: 1 skein of 29; short lengths of 225, 379, 50 and 288
- Kreinik metallic thread: 1 reel of 031
- 1 piece of 14-hole interlock canvas, 5 × 5 in (12.5 × 12.5 cm)
- Card with ready-cut mount
- Double-sided adhesive tape

1 *Follow the chart to work the design, starting in the middle (indicated by the arrows on the edges). Use half cross stitch throughout. The colours on the chart and in the key correspond with the stranded cotton and metallic thread colours and numbers.*

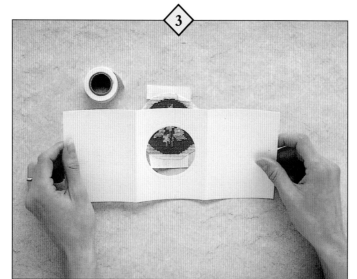

2 *After stretching the embroidery, press it with a hot steam iron over a damp cloth. Trim back the canvas.*

3 *Put a small piece of double-sided adhesive tape at the top and bottom of the embroidery and carefully centre the card mount over it.*

4 *Secure the embroidery in position with more double-sided adhesive tape and close the left-hand mount.*

TULIP CUSHION

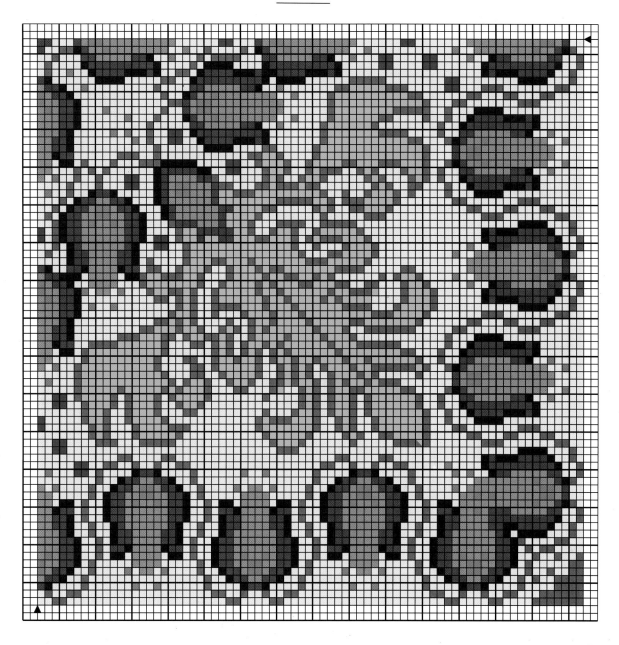

Finished size: 15 × 15 in (38 × 38 cm)

TULIP BUDS INSPIRED THE DESIGN FOR THIS CUSHION. THE MOTIF OF TULIPS AND LEAVES HAS BEEN REPEATED TO CREATE A ROUND PATTERN WITHIN A SQUARE. THE COLOURS CAN BE CHANGED TO SHADES OF YELLOW, BLUE OR RED TO SUIT YOUR OWN FURNISHINGS.

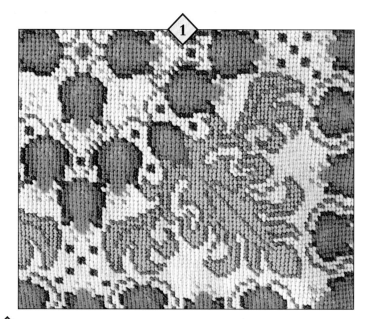

1 *Follow the chart to work the design, starting in the middle (indicated by the arrows on the edges). The chart shown here represents a quarter of the cushion. Use half cross stitch throughout. The colours on the chart and in the key correspond with the wool colours and numbers.*

KEY

	9504
	8416
	9100
	8644
	9006
	8526
	8824
	8612

MATERIALS

- Tapestry wool: 1 skein of 8824; 2 skeins of 8644; 3 skeins each of 9006, 8526, 8612; 4 skeins each of 9100, 8416; 10 skeins of 9504
- 1 piece of 10-hole, double-thread canvas, 19 × 19 in (48 × 48 cm)
- 1 piece of velvet to back, 18 in × 18 in (46 × 46 cm)
- 1 cushion pad, 15 × 15 in (38 × 38 cm)

2 *After stretching the embroidery, press it with a hot steam iron over a damp cloth. Place the embroidery and the velvet right sides together, and begin to sew them together, leaving a gap along the bottom edge for the cushion pad. Then turn the cushion right side out.*

3 *Insert the cushion pad into the cushion.*

Sew up the gap. If you wish you can add braid to match one of the colours used in the design.

SUMMER

BINDWEED DOORSTOP

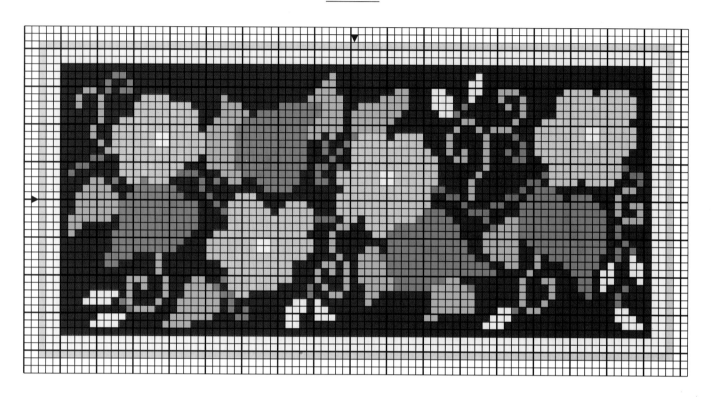

KEY

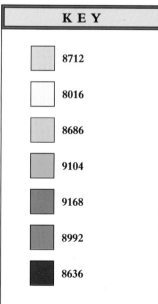

	8712
	8016
	8686
	9104
	9168
	8992
	8636

Finished size: 8⅞ × 4⅛ × 2⅞ in (22.5 × 10.5 × 7.25 cm)

AN ORDINARY STANDARD HOUSE BRICK, COVERED COMPLETELY WITH THE NEEDLEPOINT BINDWEED DESIGN, IS USED TO MAKE THIS DOORSTOP. MAKE SURE THAT YOU MEASURE THE SIZE OF THE BRICK CAREFULLY, JUST IN CASE IT IS DIFFERENT FROM THE ONE SHOWN HERE. YOU CAN MAKE THE DESIGN LARGER BY STITCHING AN EXTRA ROW OR TWO TO THE BORDER. IF YOU WANT TO DECREASE THE SIZE, THEN JUST STITCH LESS OF THE BORDER.

MATERIALS

- Tapestry wool: 1 skein of 9168; 2 skeins each of 8992, 9104 and 8686; 3 skeins of 8016; 4 skeins of 8636; short lengths of 8712
- 6 pieces of 10-hole double-thread canvas: 2 pieces 12 × 8 in (30.5 × 20.5 cm); 2 pieces 12 × 6 in (30.5 × 15 cm); 2 pieces 8 × 6 in (20.5 × 15 cm)
- Brick

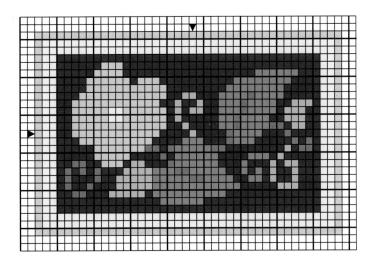

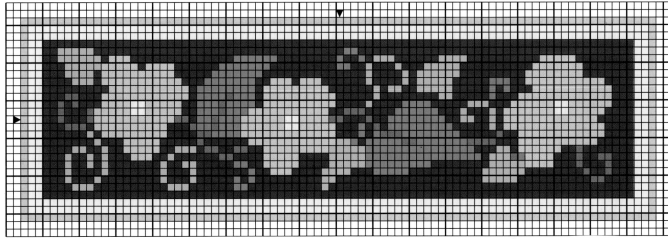

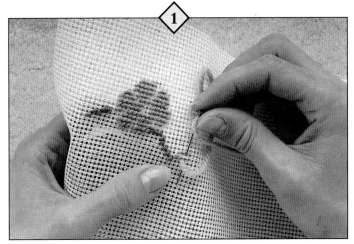

1 *Follow the chart to work the design. Use half cross stitch throughout. The colours on the charts and in the key correspond with the wool colours and numbers. Start with the flowers and their stems.*

2 *Fill in the background colour when the main design has been stitched. Stitch all the sides of the design. You will need two of each side.*

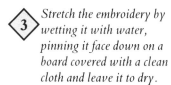

3 Stretch the embroidery by wetting it with water, pinning it face down on a board covered with a clean cloth and leave it to dry.

4 When the embroidery is dry, unpin it, press it with a hot steam iron over a damp cloth, and trim back the excess canvas, cutting the corners at an angle.

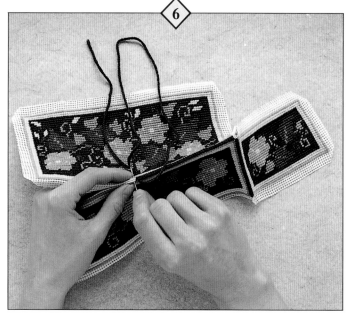

5 Stitch a side and an end together, using long-armed cross stitch.

6 Stitch the top to the sides and the bottom but leave an opening that is large enough for the brick to go in.

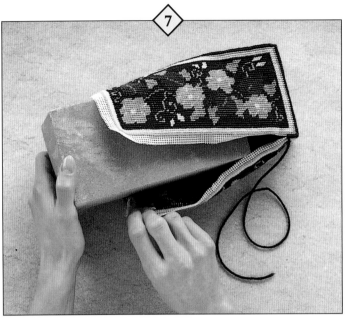

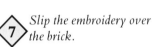
7 Slip the embroidery over the brick.

8 Stitch the open sides together using long-armed cross stitch.

POPPIES GIFT TAG

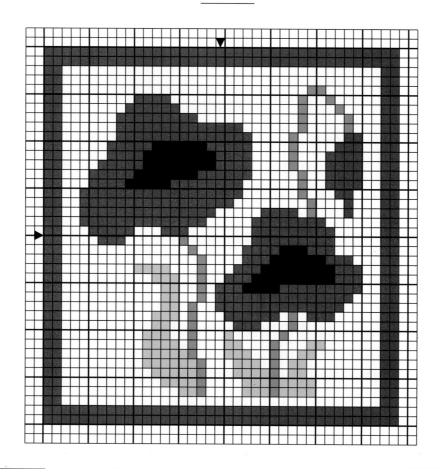

Finished size: 2¼ × 2¼ in (5.5 × 5.5 cm)

KEY	
⬜	292
▨	256
▩	258
▦	19
⬛	403

BRIGHT, CHEERFUL POPPIES ARE ALWAYS A PLEASURE TO SEE, AND THIS LITTLE GIFT TAG WILL MAKE YOUR PRESENT UNFORGETTABLE. IF YOU WANT TO MAKE A PICTURE, PINCUSHION OR NEEDLECASE, YOU CAN ADAPT THE DESIGN BY USING A LARGER MESH CANVAS.

MATERIALS

- Stranded cotton: 1 skein each of 19 and 292; short lengths of 258, 256 and 403
- 1 piece of 18-hole interlock canvas, 4 × 4 in (10 × 10 cm)
- Cardboard to back
- 1 piece of lining fabric, 3 × 3 in (7.5 × 7.5 cm)
- Ribbon
- Small adhesive address label

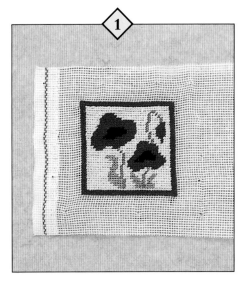

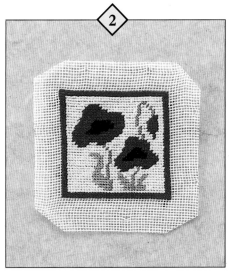

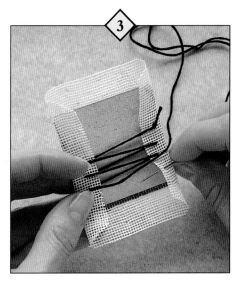

1 *Follow the chart to work the design, starting in the middle (indicated by the arrows on the edges). Use half cross stitch throughout. The colours on the chart and in the key correspond with the stranded cotton colours and numbers.*

2 *After stretching the embroidery, press it with a hot steam iron over a damp cloth, and trim back the canvas, cutting the corners at an angle.*

3 *Cut a piece of cardboard slightly smaller than the embroidery and lace the edges together, stitching first from side to side, then from top to bottom.*

4 *Line the back and then sew on a piece of ribbon.*

5 *Add a label on which you can write your message. An adhesive label has been used here, but you can back the tag with any card.*

BUSY LIZZIE
CALENDAR

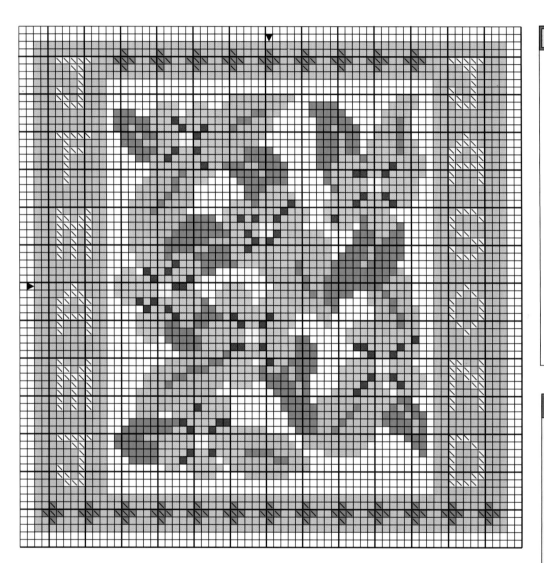

MATERIALS

- Tapestry wool: 1 skein each of 8006 and 8992; 2 skeins of 9002; short lengths of 8432, 8490 and 8112
- 1 piece of 10-hole, double-thread canvas, 9 × 9 in (23 × 23 cm)
- Piece of cardboard to mount the finished embroidery
- 1 piece of lining fabric 7½ × 7½ in (18 × 18 cm)
- Ribbon
- Calendar

Finished size: 6½ × 6½ in (16.5 × 16.5 cm)

THE INITIALS OF THE MONTHS OF THE YEAR HAVE BEEN STITCHED IN CROSS STITCH TO MAKE A PRETTY BORDER FOR THIS CALENDAR. IF YOU PREFER, YOU CAN STITCH A CHILD'S NAME INSTEAD AND, PERHAPS, ADD THE DATE OF BIRTH.

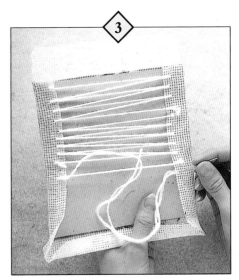

1 Follow the chart to work the design, starting in the middle (indicated by the arrows on the edges). The colours on the chart and in the key correspond with the wool colours and numbers. The letters down the side of the calendar and the dark green motifs along the top and bottom have been stitched in cross stitch. The top of the cross lies in the opposite direction to the rest of the work.

2 After stretching the embroidery, press it with a hot steam iron over a damp cloth, and trim back the canvas, cutting the corners at an angle.

3 Cut a piece of cardboard slightly smaller than the finished embroidery and lace the edges of the sides together, going first from side to side, then from top to bottom. Add a ribbon loop at the top and a calendar attached to a length of ribbon at the bottom.

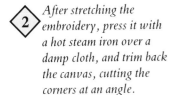

Calendar

S T R A W B E R R Y A N D
F O R G E T - M E - N O T
P I N C U S H I O N

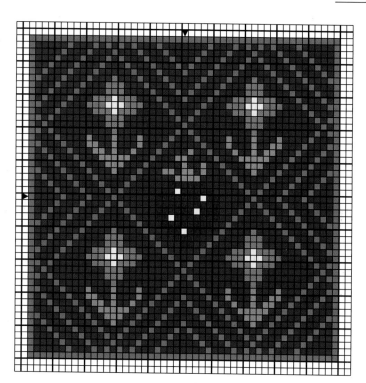
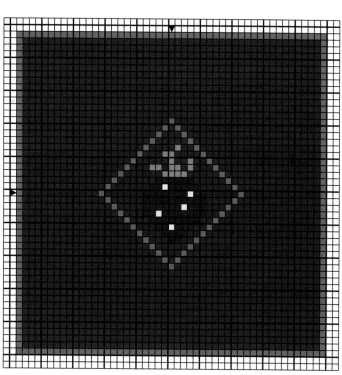

KEY

	8114
	8644
	9018
	8218
	9006
	8740

Finished size: 4 × 4 in (10 × 10 cm)

THE BRIGHT RED OF THE STRAWBERRY AND THE PRETTY BLUE OF THE FORGET-ME-NOTS MAKE THIS A LOVELY PROJECT TO WORK. THE DESIGN CAN BE ADAPTED TO MAKE A COORDINATING NEEDLECASE SIMPLY BY USING A 10-HOLE, DOUBLE-THREAD CANVAS.

MATERIALS

- Tapestry wool: 1 skein of 9006; 3 skeins of 8740; short lengths of 8218, 8114, 8644 and 9018
- 2 pieces of 12-hole interlock canvas, each 7 × 7 in (17.5 × 17.5 cm)
- Polyester toy stuffing

1 *Follow the chart to work the design, starting in the middle (indicated by the arrows on the edges). Use half cross stitch throughout. The colours on the charts and in the key correspond with the wool colours and numbers.*

2 *After stretching the embroidery, press it with a hot steam iron over a damp cloth, and trim back the canvas, cutting the corners at an angle.*

3 *Stitch the two sides together, wrong sides facing, using long-armed cross stitch. Leave a small gap along one of the sides.*

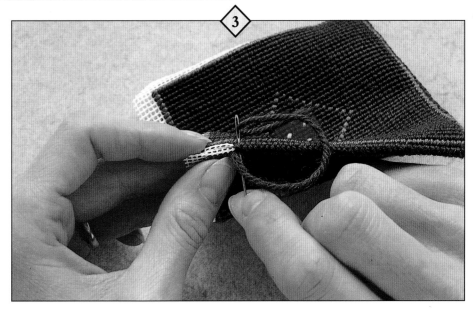

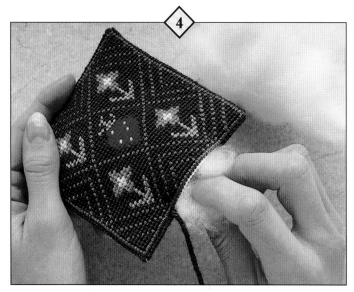

4 ◈ *Stuff the pincushion with polyester toy stuffing.*

5 ◈ *Stitch the gap together.*

S W E E T P E A   C A R D

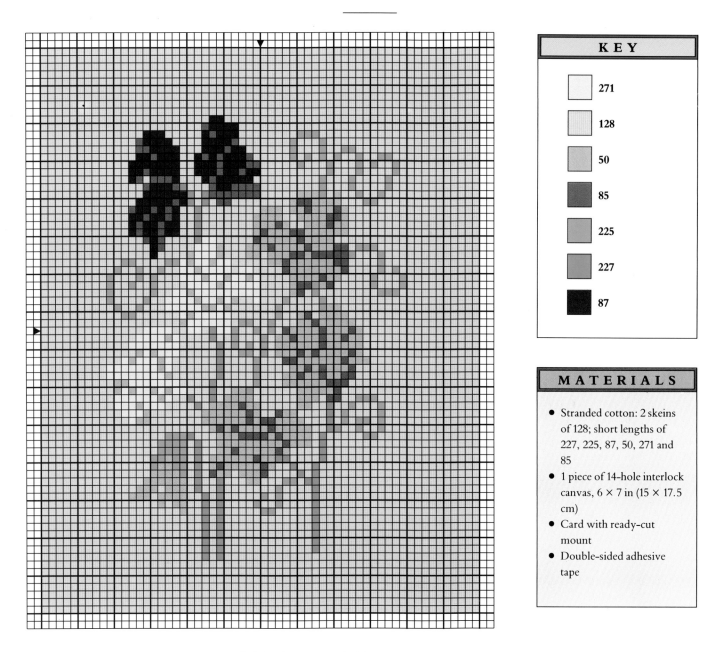

KEY

☐	271
☐	128
☐	50
☐	85
☐	225
☐	227
■	87

MATERIALS

- Stranded cotton: 2 skeins of 128; short lengths of 227, 225, 87, 50, 271 and 85
- 1 piece of 14-hole interlock canvas, 6 × 7 in (15 × 17.5 cm)
- Card with ready-cut mount
- Double-sided adhesive tape

Finished size: oval 3¾ × 4¾ in (9.5 × 12 cm)

THIS CHARMING DESIGN CAPTURES THE WARMTH OF SUMMER, AND IT WOULD MAKE AN IDEAL CARD FOR A BIRTHDAY OR WEDDING. IF YOU PREFER IT CAN JUST AS EASILY BE FRAMED AND MADE INTO A PICTURE AND YOU CAN USE A MOUNT OF COLOURED CARD TO HIGHLIGHT ONE OF THE PINK SHADES. GREETINGS CARDS FOR MOUNTING EMBROIDERY ARE AVAILABLE FROM NEEDLECRAFT AND HABERDASHERY SHOPS.

1 *Follow the chart to work the design, starting in the middle (indicated by the arrows on the edges). Use half cross stitch throughout. The colours on the chart and in the key correspond with the stranded cotton colours and numbers.*

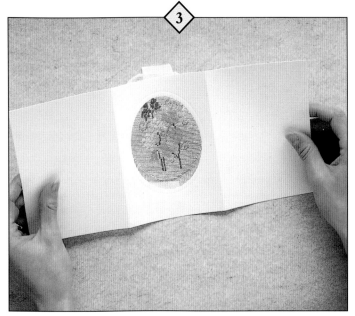

2 *After stretching the embroidery, press it with a hot steam iron over a damp cloth, and trim back the canvas.*

3 *Put a small piece of double-sided adhesive tape at the top and bottom of the embroidery and carefully centre the card mount. Secure the embroidery in position with more double-sided adhesive tape.*

4 *Peel off the top of the tape and close the left side of the card mount, which acts as a backing.*

HIBISCUS PATCH

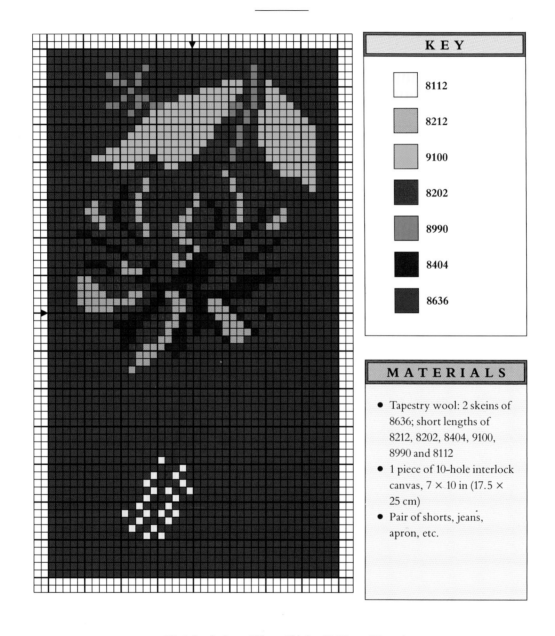

KEY	
☐	8112
▨	8212
▨	9100
▨	8202
▨	8990
■	8404
▨	8636

MATERIALS

- Tapestry wool: 2 skeins of 8636; short lengths of 8212, 8202, 8404, 9100, 8990 and 8112
- 1 piece of 10-hole interlock canvas, 7 × 10 in (17.5 × 25 cm)
- Pair of shorts, jeans, apron, etc.

Finished size: 3⅞ × 6¾ in (9.75 × 17 cm)

ADDING EMBROIDERED PATCHES TO CLOTHING IS ALWAYS POPULAR, AND THIS HIBISCUS DESIGN CAN BE USED TO MAKE A FUN EMBLEM ON A PAIR OF SHORTS. IF YOU BACK THE PATCH WITH SOME LINING FABRIC AND LEAVE THE TOP OPEN WHEN YOU SEW IT ONTO THE SHORTS, YOU CAN MAKE A POCKET.

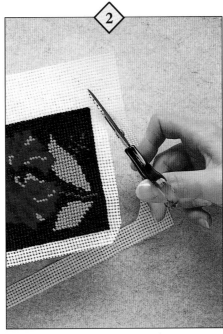

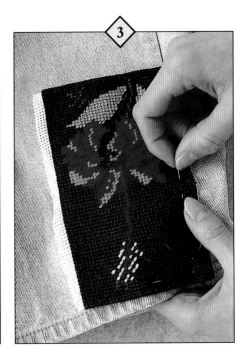

1 Follow the chart to work the design, starting in the middle (indicated by the arrows on the edges). Use half cross stitch throughout. The colours on the chart and in the key correspond with the wool colours and numbers.

2 After stretching the embroidery, press it with a hot steam iron over a damp cloth, and trim back the canvas, cutting the corners at an angle.

3 Pin the patch into position on a pair of shorts or jeans or on an apron, etc.

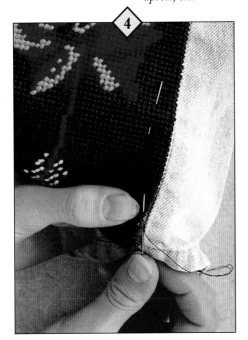

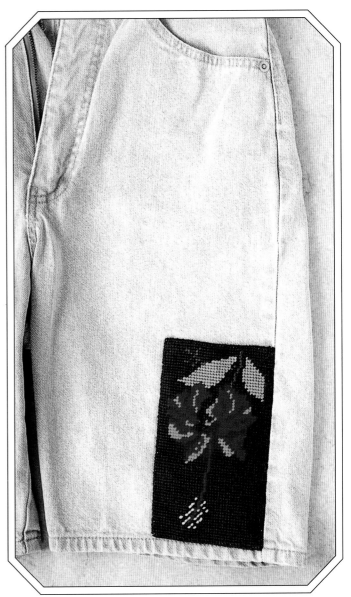

4 Carefully sew it in place, using slip stitch.

F U C H S I A
S P E C T A C L E S   C A S E

KEY

☐	8006
▨	9002
▨	8490
▨	8202
▨	8992
▨	8218

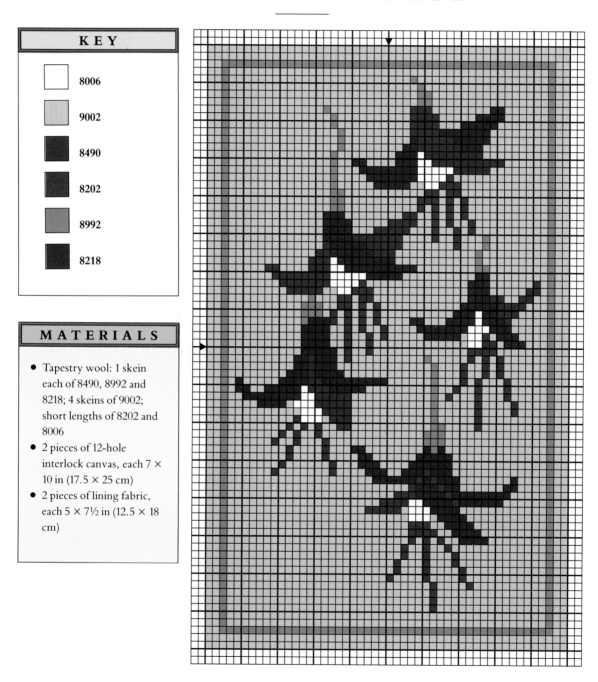

MATERIALS

- Tapestry wool: 1 skein each of 8490, 8992 and 8218; 4 skeins of 9002; short lengths of 8202 and 8006
- 2 pieces of 12-hole interlock canvas, each 7 × 10 in (17.5 × 25 cm)
- 2 pieces of lining fabric, each 5 × 7½ in (12.5 × 18 cm)

Finished size: 4¼ × 6¾ in (10.5 × 17 cm)

THE BRILLIANT COLOURS OF FUCHSIAS ARE IDEAL FOR A NEEDLEPOINT PROJECT. I HAVE CHOSEN TO USE THIS DESIGN ON A SPECTACLES CASE, BUT YOU CAN ADAPT IT TO MAKE A BOOKMARK OR, IF YOU USE A SOFTER CREAMY BACKGROUND COLOUR, A PICTURE.

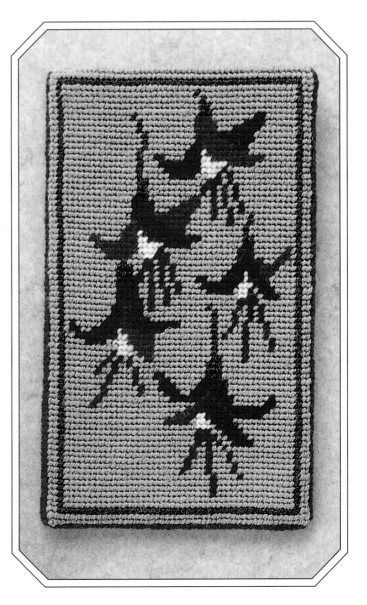

 Follow the chart to work the design, starting in the middle (indicated by the arrows on the edges). Use half cross stitch throughout. The colours on the chart and in the key correspond with the wool colours and numbers. After stretching the embroidery, press it with a hot steam iron over a damp cloth, and trim back the canvas, cutting the corners at an angle.

 Line each side with some pretty fabric.

Stitch the front and back together, using long-armed cross stitch in a contrasting colour. Leave the top open.

DOG ROSE
PINCUSHION

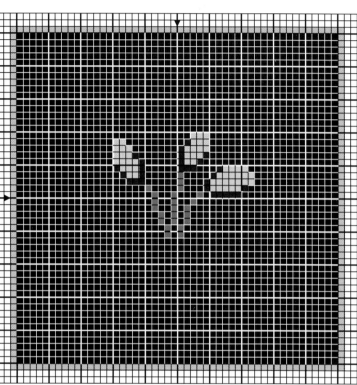

KEY	
	8006
	8392
	8396
	8016
	9100
	8042
	9006
	9800

Finished size: 4½ × 4½ in (11 × 11 cm)

THE PRETTY COLOURS OF WILD ROSES HAVE INSPIRED SOME LOVELY NEEDLEPOINT DESIGNS. THIS MOTIF HAS BEEN CREATED FOR A PINCUSHION, BUT IF YOU USE A LARGER MESH CANVAS IT CAN EASILY BE MADE INTO A PICTURE OR A SMALL HERB SACHET.

MATERIALS

- Tapestry wool: 1 skein of 8396; 3 skeins of 9800; short lengths of 8392, 8042, 8006, 8016, 9100 and 9006
- 2 pieces of 12-hole interlock canvas, each 7 × 7 in (17.5 × 17.5 cm)
- Polyester toy stuffing

1 *Follow the chart to work the design, starting in the middle (indicated by the arrows on the edges). Use half cross stitch throughout. The colours on the charts and in the key correspond with the wool colours and numbers.*

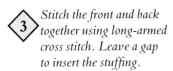

2 *After stretching the embroidery, press it with a hot steam iron over a damp cloth, and trim back the canvas, cutting the corners at an angle.*

3 *Stitch the front and back together using long-armed cross stitch. Leave a gap to insert the stuffing.*

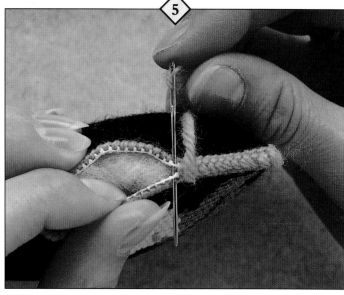

4 Stuff the pincushion with polyester toy stuffing.

5 Sew up the gap.

ACORN BOX

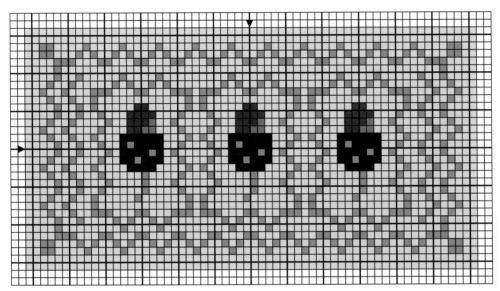

MATERIALS

- Tapestry wool: 1 skein each of 9642, 9216 and 8312; 2 skeins of 959 ; 6 skeins of 8254
- 2 sheets of 10-hole clear plastic canvas, each 11 × 14 in (28 × 35 cm)
- 2 pieces of lining fabric, 7½ × 4½ in (18 × 11 cm); 2 pieces 7½ × 4 in (18 × 10 cm); 2 pieces 4½ × 4 in (11 × 10 cm)

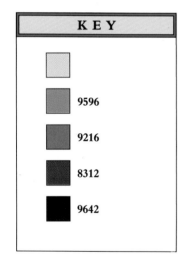

KEY	
	9596
	9216
	8312
	9642

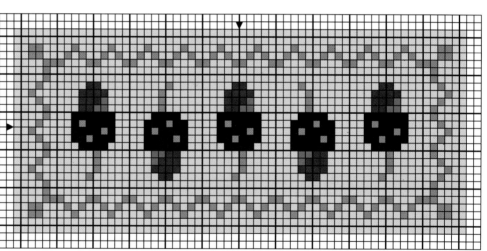

Finished size: 6½ × 3½ × 3 in (16.5 × 9 × 7.5 cm)

PLASTIC CANVAS IS RIGID ENOUGH TO MAKE A BOX THAT CAN BE USED TO HOLD ALL SORTS OF BITS AND PIECES. THE DESIGN IS WORKED ON 10-HOLE PLASTIC CANVAS, WHICH ALLOWS IT TO BE MORE DETAILED.

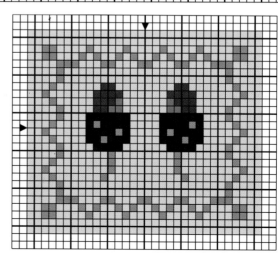

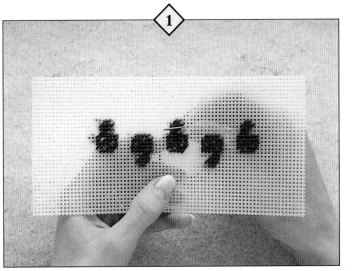

1 Follow the chart to work the design, starting in the middle of each side (indicated by the arrows on the edges). The sides (middle and bottom charts) are all stitched separately. The top of the box is the top chart. Use half cross stitch

throughout except for the bottom of the box which is plain and stitched in cross stitch. The colours on the charts and in the key correspond with the wool colours and numbers. Start with the acorns themselves.

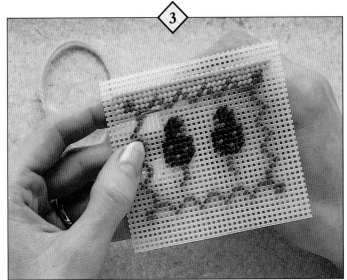

2 Stitch the main design, then fill in the background.

3 Work the short sides in the same way as the long sides.

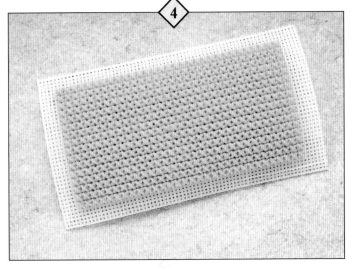

4 The base of the box is stitched in cross stitch over two holes. This is quicker to work but also covers the plastic canvas very well.

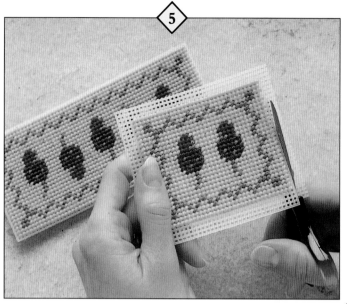

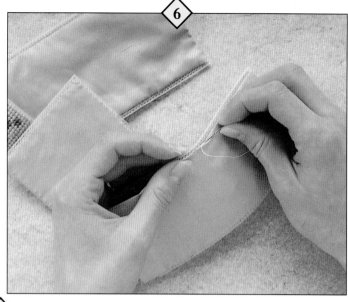

5 Trim back the excess canvas on all sides. There is no need to block plastic canvas.

6 Line each of the four sides.

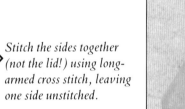

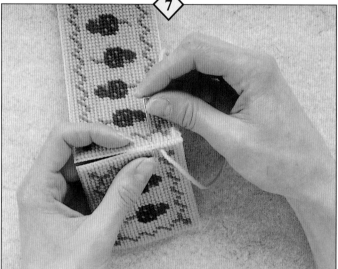

7 Stitch the sides together (not the lid!) using long-armed cross stitch, leaving one side unstitched.

8 Stitch the sides to the bottom and then stitch the final side.

9 Overstitch the edges along the top of the box using the pinky background wool.

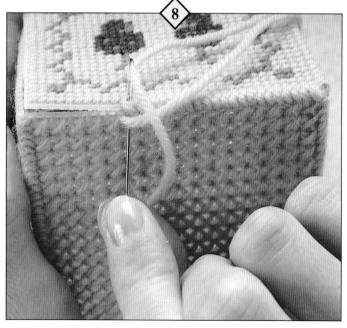

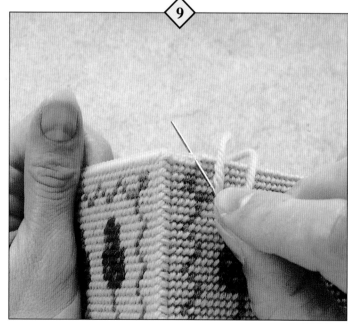

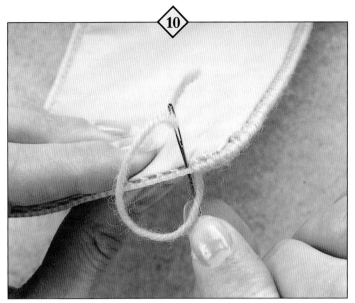

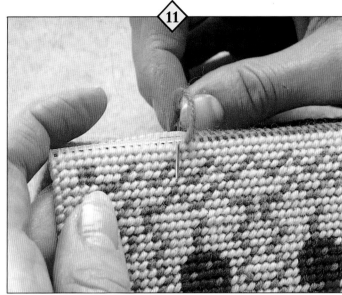

◆10◆ *Overstitch around three sides of the lid of the box.*

◆11◆ *Stitch the lid to the box using an overstitch in a contrasting wool.*

R O S E H I P   K E Y   R I N G

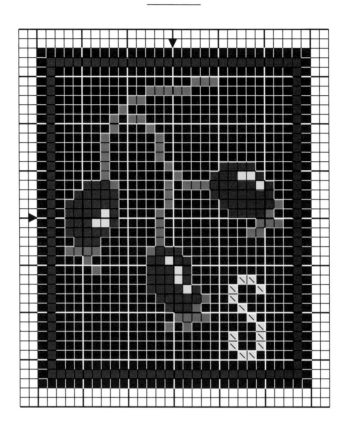

K E Y

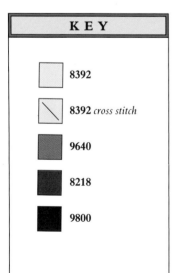

8392

8392 *cross stitch*

9640

8218

9800

Finished size: 2½ × 3 in (6.5 × 7.5 cm)

WHEN YOU ARE IN A HURRY THERE'S NOTHING WORSE THAN FORGETTING WHERE YOU HAVE PUT YOUR KEYS, BUT THIS PRETTY KEY RING FOB WILL HELP YOU KEEP TRACK OF THEM. YOU CAN ADD ANY INITIAL IN THE CORNER, USING CROSS STITCH TO MAKE THE STITCHES LOOK SQUARE.

M A T E R I A L S

- Tapestry wool: 1 skein of 9800; short lengths of 8218, 8392 and 9640
- 1 piece of 12-hole interlock canvas, 5 × 6 in (12.5 × 15 cm)
- Cardboard for backing
- 1 piece of lining fabric, 3½ × 4 in (9 × 10 in)
- Ribbon
- Key ring

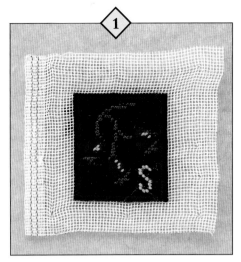

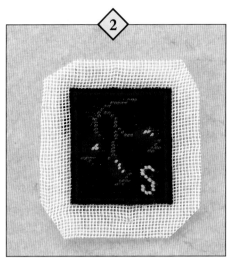

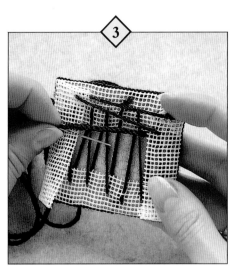

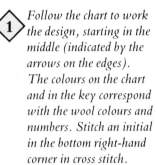 1 Follow the chart to work the design, starting in the middle (indicated by the arrows on the edges). The colours on the chart and in the key correspond with the wool colours and numbers. Stitch an initial in the bottom right-hand corner in cross stitch.

2 After stretching the embroidery, press it with a hot steam iron over a damp cloth, and trim back the canvas, cutting the corners at an angle.

3 Cut a piece of board slightly smaller than the finished embroidery and lace the edges of the excess canvas together, working first from side to side, then from top to bottom.

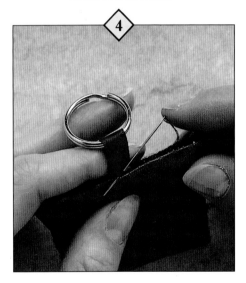

4 Line the back carefully, adding a piece of ribbon with a keyring attached to the top of the key fob.

CRAB APPLE BOOKMARK

Finished size: 1 × 7 in (2.5 × 17.5 cm)

THIS PRETTY BOOKMARK IS IDEAL FOR MARKING THE PLACE IN YOUR FAVOURITE COOKERY OR GARDENING BOOK. THE DESIGN CAN BE EASILY ADAPTED TO MAKE A LITTLE BELLPULL BY STITCHING ANOTHER ROW OF CRAB APPLES ALONGSIDE AND MAKING THE BORDER ONE OR TWO ROWS LARGER.

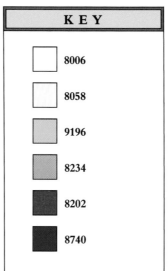

KEY

	8006
	8058
	9196
	8234
	8202
	8740

MATERIALS

- Tapestry wool: 1 skein of 8740; short lengths of 8058, 8234, 8202, 9196 and 8006
- 1 piece of 12-hole interlock canvas, 4 × 10 in (10 × 25 cm)
- 1 piece of lining fabric, 2 × 8 in (5 × 20.5 cm)
- Tassel

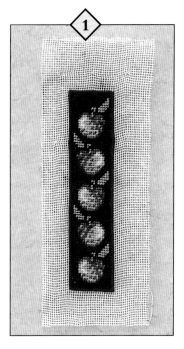

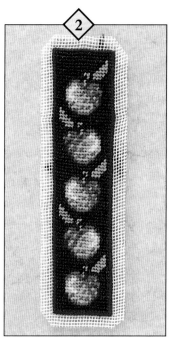

1 *Follow the chart to work the design, starting in the middle (indicated by the arrows on the edges). Use half cross stitch throughout. The colours on the chart and in the key correspond with the wool colours and numbers.*

2 *After stretching the embroidery, press it with a hot steam iron over a damp cloth, and trim back the canvas, cutting the corners at an angle.*

3 *Sew a piece of pretty fabric to the back of the embroidery, and press it with a hot steam iron over* *a damp cloth. Sew a tassel to the bottom edge of the bookmark to complete it.*

G R A P E
M I R R O R   C A S E

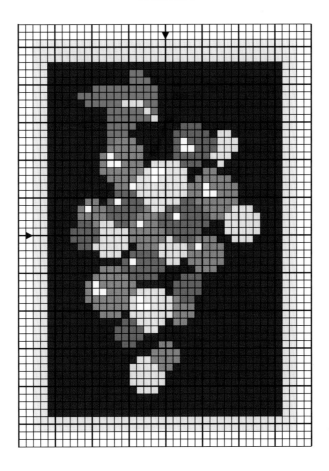

Finished size: 3 × 4½ in (7.5 × 11 cm)

THIS CHARMING LITTLE DESIGN MAKES A PRETTY CASE FOR A HANDBAG MIRROR. YOU CAN ADAPT THE DESIGN TO MAKE A SMALL EVENING PURSE, ADDING A ZIP ACROSS THE TOP AND PERHAPS PUTTING A FEW BEADS ON THE GRAPES. USE A METALLIC THREAD IN THE BACKGROUND TO MAKE IT SPARKLE.

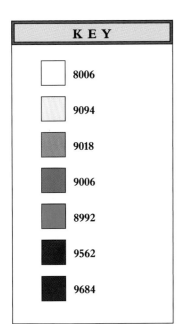

KEY	
☐	8006
☐	9094
☐	9018
☐	9006
☐	8992
☐	9562
☐	9684

MATERIALS

- Tapestry wool: 1 skein of 9094; 2 skeins of 9684; short lengths of 9018, 9006, 8992, 9562 and 8006
- 2 pieces of 12-hole interlock canvas, each 6 × 8 in (15 × 20.5 cm)
- 2 pieces of lining fabric, each 4 × 5½ in (10 × 14 cm)

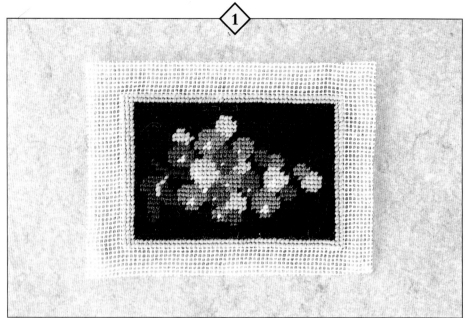

1 *Follow the chart to work the design, starting in the middle (indicated by the arrows on the edges). Use half cross stitch throughout. The colours on the chart and in the key correspond with the wool colours and numbers. Stitch two pieces, one for the front and one for the back.*

2 *After stretching the embroidery, press it with a hot steam iron over a damp cloth, and trim back the canvas, cutting the corners at an angle.*

3 *Line each side with a piece of fabric.*

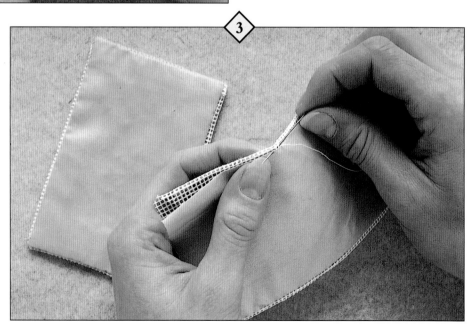

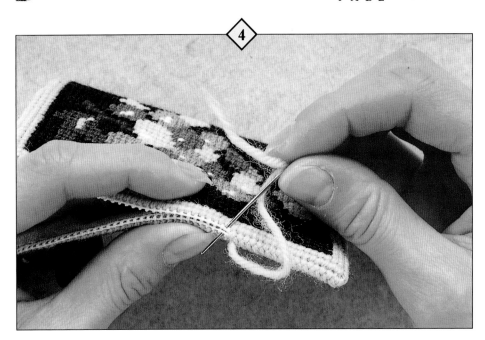

◆ **4** Stitch the two sides
together with long-armed
cross stitch. Press with a
hot steam iron over a
damp cloth.

B L A C K B E R R Y
C O M B C A S E

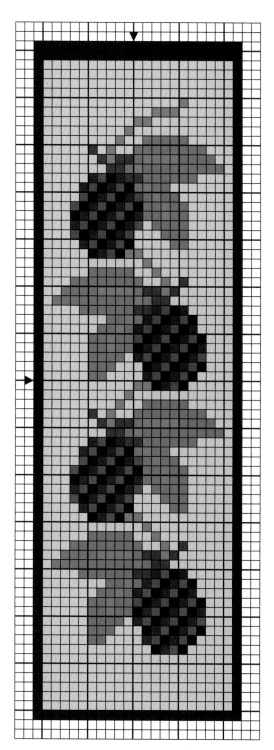

Finished size: 2 × 6 in (5 × 15 cm)

THIS COMB CASE WILL BE A PRETTY AND USEFUL
ACCESSORY FOR YOUR HANDBAG, AND YOU CAN
ADAPT THE DESIGN TO MAKE A COORDINATING
MIRROR CASE, LIPSTICK HOLDER AND MUCH MORE.
EXPERIMENT WITH THE MOTIF BY USING LARGER
CANVAS OR FINE EVENWEAVE FABRIC AND DELICATE
COTTONS, AND ADD BEADS OR METALLIC THREADS
FOR EVENING USE.

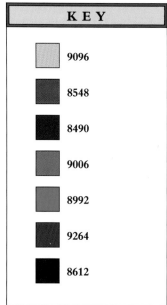

KEY	
	9096
	8548
	8490
	9006
	8992
	9264
	8612

M A T E R I A L S

- Tapestry wool: 1 skein each of 9096 and 9006; short lengths of 9264, 8992, 8490, 8548 and 8612
- 2 pieces of 12-hole interlock canvas, each 5 × 9 in (12.5 × 23 cm)
- 2 pieces of lining fabric, each 3 × 7 in (7.5 × 17.5 cm)

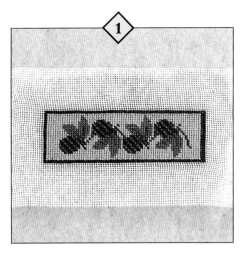

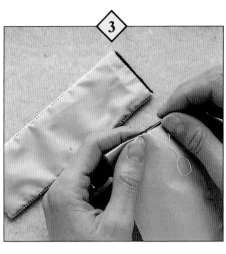

1 *Follow the chart to work the design, starting in the middle (indicated by the arrows on the edges). Use half cross stitch throughout. The colours on the chart and in the key correspond with the wool colours and numbers. Work two pieces, one for the front and one for the back.*

3 *Sew a piece of lining fabric to each side.*

4 *Stitch the front and back together using long-armed cross stitch and press with a hot steam iron over a damp cloth.*

2 *After stretching the embroidery, press it with a hot steam iron over a damp cloth, and trim back the canvas, cutting the corners at an angle.*

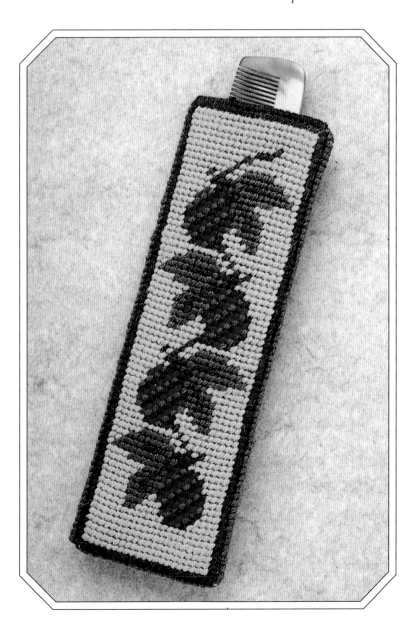

L A V E N D E R   S A C H E T

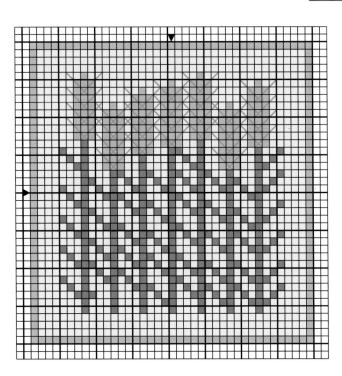

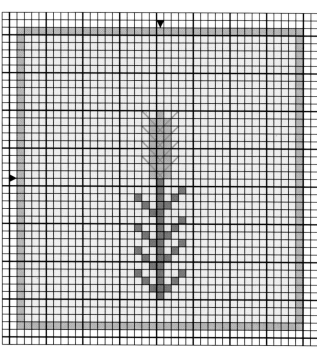

KEY	
⬜	8296
⬛	8604
⬛	9076
∿	108

Finished size: 3¼ × 3¼ in (8 × 8 cm)

THIS LITTLE LAVENDER SACHET IS PERFECT FOR SCENTING A WARDROBE OR DRAWER. USING STRANDED COTTON TO OVERSTITCH THE LAVENDER HEADS GIVES A DELICATE FEEL TO THE DESIGN, AND THE LACE EDGING ADDS THAT EXTRA TOUCH OF LUXURY.

MATERIALS

- Tapestry wool: 1 skein each of 8604 and 9076; 2 skeins of 8296
- Stranded cotton: short length of 108
- 2 pieces of 12-hole interlock canvas, each 6 × 6 in (15 × 15 cm)
- Polyester toy stuffing
- Dried lavender
- Lace

1 *Follow the chart to work the design, starting in the middle (indicated by the arrows on the edges). Use half cross stitch throughout. The colours on the charts and in the key correspond with the wool and stranded cotton colours and numbers. There is one design for the front and one for the back. After stitching the needlepoint, use the stranded cotton to oversew the details on the lavender heads.*

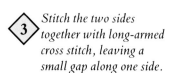

2 *After stretching the embroidery, press it with a hot steam iron over a damp cloth, and trim back the canvas, cutting the corners at an angle.*

3 *Stitch the two sides together with long-armed cross stitch, leaving a small gap along one side.*

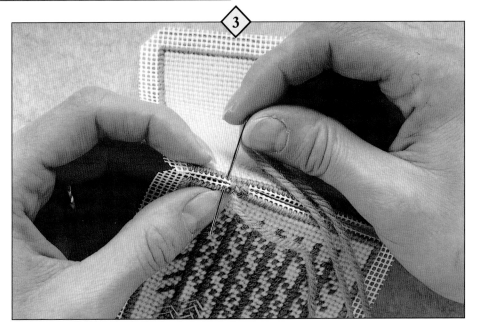

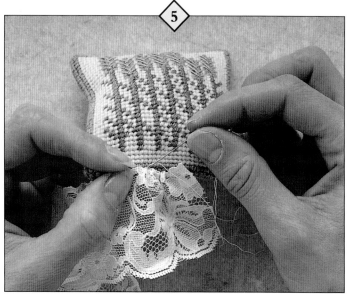

4 *Stuff the sachet with polyester toy stuffing and some dried lavender.*

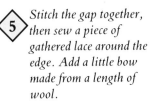

5 *Stitch the gap together, then sew a piece of gathered lace around the edge. Add a little bow made from a length of wool.*

WINTER

P O I N S E T T I A
H E R B   S A C H E T

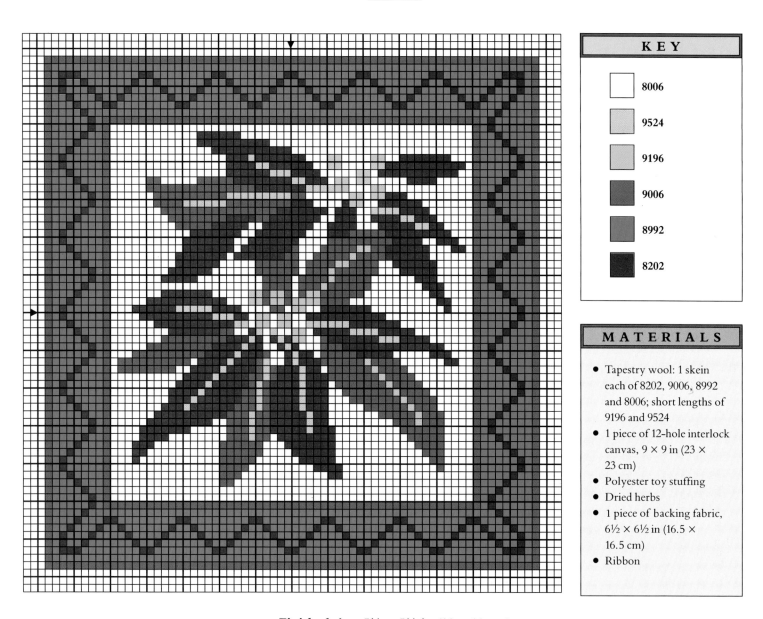

KEY

⬜	8006
◻	9524
◻	9196
◼	9006
◼	8992
◼	8202

MATERIALS

- Tapestry wool: 1 skein each of 8202, 9006, 8992 and 8006; short lengths of 9196 and 9524
- 1 piece of 12-hole interlock canvas, 9 × 9 in (23 × 23 cm)
- Polyester toy stuffing
- Dried herbs
- 1 piece of backing fabric, 6½ × 6½ in (16.5 × 16.5 cm)
- Ribbon

Finished size: 5½ × 5½ in (14 × 14 cm)

POINSETTIAS ARE FAVOURITE PLANTS IN THE WINTER MONTHS, BRIGHTENING OUR DULL ROOMS WITH THEIR CHEERFUL RED LEAVES. THE DESIGN FOR THIS HERB SACHET WAS INSPIRED BY THE COLOURS AND SHAPES OF THE POINSETTIA, AND IT WILL ADD A TOUCH OF BRIGHTNESS TO A CORNER OF YOUR HOME.

1 *Follow the chart to work the design, starting in the middle (indicated by the arrows on the edges). Use half cross stitch throughout. The colours on the chart and in the key correspond with the wool colours and numbers. Begin with the red leaves and then stitch the green border line.*

1

2

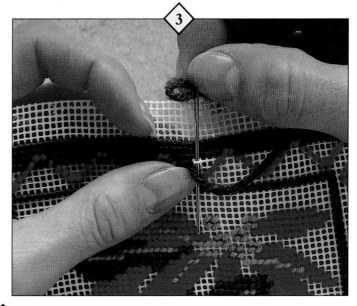

3

2 *Stitch the rest of the leaves in green, then work the red zigzag border.*

3 *Fill in the green border area and the smaller details in the design.*

4

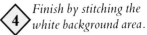

4 *Finish by stitching the white background area.*

5 Dampen the embroidery with water and pin it, face down, on a covered board.

6 When the embroidery is dry, unpin it and press it with a hot steam iron over a damp cloth; trim back the canvas, cutting the corners at an angle.

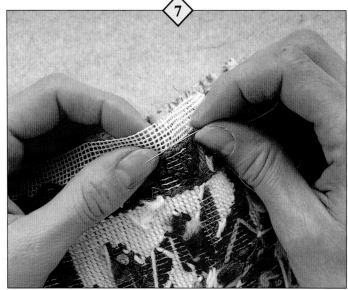

7 Carefully sew on the backing fabric, right sides together, leaving a gap for the stuffing.

8 Turn the sachet the right way out.

 9 Stuff the sachet with polyester toy stuffing and some dried herbs.

 10 Sew the gap together and add a bright red ribbon to finish.

HOLLY GIFT TAG

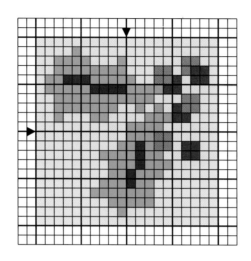

Finished size: 3¾ × 3¾ in (9.5 × 9.5 cm)

THIS MOTIF HAS BEEN STITCHED ON PLASTIC CANVAS TO GIVE A NICE RIGID SHAPE. IT IS QUICK AND EASY TO CREATE AND MAKES GIVING A PRESENT THAT EXTRA BIT SPECIAL. A SMALL BOX CAN BE MADE USING THIS DESIGN BY STITCHING FIVE SIDES WITH THIS MOTIF AND ONE SIDE PLAIN FOR THE BOTTOM.

KEY

	998
	253
	676
	901
	686

MATERIALS

- Plastic canvas yarn: 1 skein of 998; short lengths of 676, 686, 253 and 901
- 1 piece of 7-hole clear plastic canvas, 6 × 6 in (15 × 15 cm)
- 1 piece of lining fabric, 5 × 5 in (12.5 × 12.5 cm)
- Ribbon
- Address label

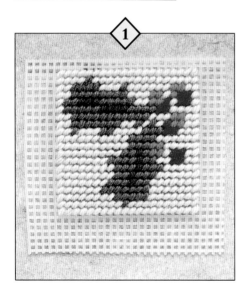

1 *Follow the chart to work the design, starting in the middle (indicated by the arrows on the edges). Use half cross stitch throughout. The colours on the chart and in the key correspond with the yarn colours and numbers.*

2 *Trim the excess canvas. There is no need to block plastic canvas.*

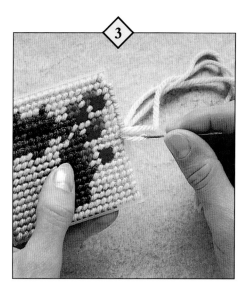

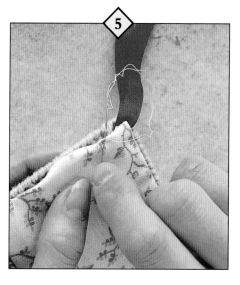

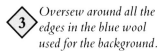

3 Oversew around all the edges in the blue wool used for the background.

4 Line the back so that the ends are covered, leaving a gap at the top right-hand corner.

5 Add a piece of ribbon to the top right-hand corner, cover with the lining fabric and then finish sewing up the lining fabric. An adhesive label can also be stuck to the back.

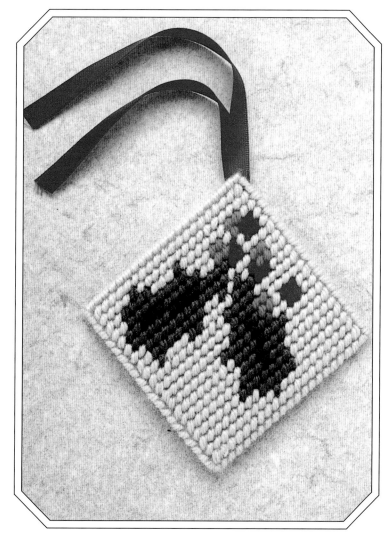

MISTLETOE CHRISTMAS DECORATION

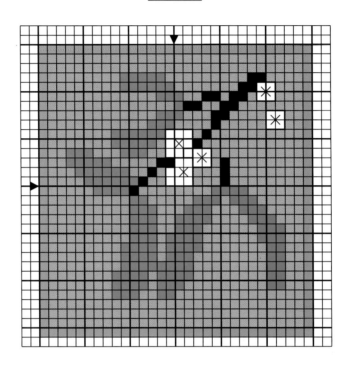

Finished size: 2½ × 2½ in (6.5 × 6.5 cm)

THIS CHRISTMAS DECORATION IS SOMETHING YOU WILL BE ABLE TO USE YEAR AFTER YEAR TO HANG ON THE TREE OR OVER THE MANTELPIECE. IF YOU WORK THE DESIGN ON LARGER MESH CANVAS AND LEAVE THE TOP EDGE OPEN, YOU CAN MAKE A LITTLE POUCH TO HOLD A SPECIAL PRESENT.

MATERIALS

- Tapestry wool: 1 skein of 8232; short lengths of 8990, 9800, 8006 and 9100
- 2 pieces of 12-hole interlock canvas, each 5 × 5 in (12.5 × 12.5 cm)
- 10 gold beads
- Polyester toy stuffing

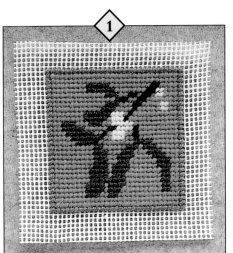

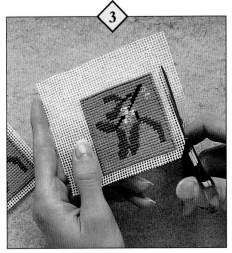

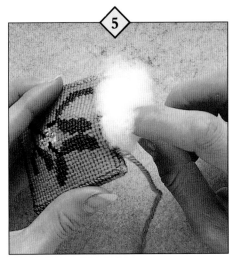

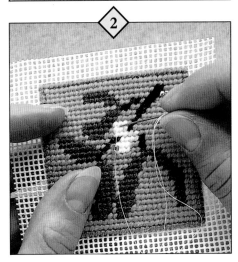

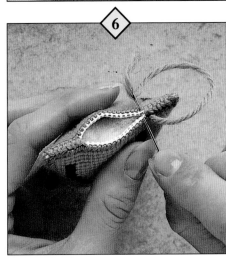

1 Follow the chart to work the design, starting in the middle (indicated by the arrows on the edges). Use half cross stitch throughout. The colours on the chart and in the key correspond with the wool colours and numbers. Stitch two pieces the same.

2 Add the beads to the embroidery.

3 After stretching the embroidery, press it with a hot steam iron over a damp cloth, and trim back the canvas, cutting the corners at an angle.

4 Stitch the two sides together with long-armed cross stitch, leaving a gap for the stuffing.

5 Stuff the decoration.

6 Stitch the gap together. Add a length of wool sewn through the edge of the decoration and tie the ends into a bow.

IVY NAPKIN RING

Finished size: 2 × 7¼ in (5 × 18 cm)

ALTHOUGH IVY IS TRADITIONALLY ASSOCIATED WITH
THE COLDER WINTER MONTHS, THE GLOSSY GREEN
LEAVES ARE FOUND THROUGHOUT THE YEAR. USING
A PINK BACKGROUND FOR THIS NAPKIN RING MEANS
THAT IT CAN BE USED BOTH IN SUMMER AND WINTER.
ALTERNATIVELY YOU CAN CHOOSE A BACKGROUND
COLOUR THAT MATCHES YOUR DINNER SERVICE.

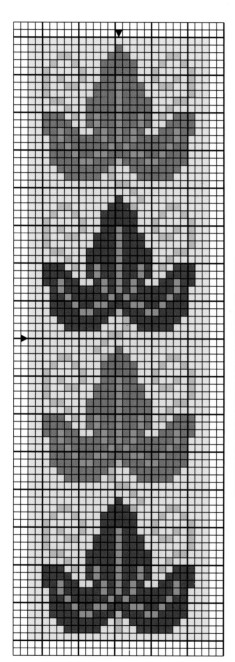

KEY	
	8392
	256
	257
	9076
	9022

MATERIALS

- Tapestry wool: 1 skein of
  8392; short lengths of 9076
  and 9022
- Stranded cotton: 1 skein
  each of 256 and 257
- 1 piece of 12-hole interlock
  canvas, 5 × 10 in (12.5 ×
  20 cm)
- 1 piece of lining fabric,
  3 × 8½ in (7.5 × 22 cm)

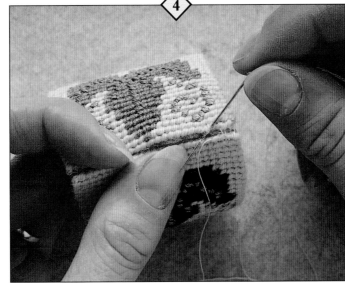

1 *Follow the chart to work the design, starting in the middle (indicated by the arrows on the edges). The colours on the chart and in the key correspond with the wool and stranded cotton colours and numbers. The wool has been stitched in half cross stitch, while the stranded cotton has been stitched in cross stitch.*

3 *Carefully sew a piece of pretty fabric to the back.*

4 *Press with a hot steam iron over a damp cloth and carefully sew the ends together using a fine cotton overstitch.*

2 *After stretching the embroidery, press it with a hot steam iron over a damp cloth, and trim back the canvas, cutting the corners at an angle.*

ROBIN AND
SNOWDROPS
PICTURE

KEY	
☐	8006
☐	8058
☐	8684
▨	9100
▨	8202
■	9640
■	9662
■	9800

MATERIALS

- Tapestry wool: 1 skein of 9640; 2 skeins each of 8006 and 8684; short lengths of 8202, 8058, 9800, 9662 and 9100
- 1 piece of 10-hole, double-thread canvas, 9 × 9 in (23 × 23 cm)
- Cardboard for backing
- Ribbon

Finished size: 6½ × 6¼ in (16.5 × 16 cm)

THIS IS A LITTLE PICTURE A CHILD WILL TREASURE FOR MANY YEARS. IT IS QUICK TO STITCH, AND IF YOU HAVE IT PROFESSIONALLY MOUNTED IN A WOODEN FRAME IT WILL MAKE AN EXTRA SPECIAL PRESENT.

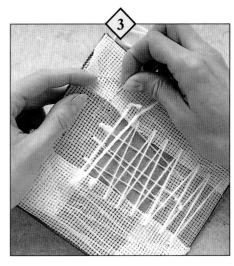

1 Follow the chart to work the design, starting in the middle (indicated by the arrows on the edges). Use half cross stitch throughout. The colours on the chart and in the key correspond with the wool colours and numbers.

2 After stretching the embroidery, press it with a hot steam iron over a damp cloth, and trim back the canvas, cutting the corners at an angle.

3 Cut a piece of board slightly smaller than the embroidery, then lace the edges of the canvas together, working first from side to side, then from top to bottom. Add a piece of ribbon to make a loop at the top and make a small bow and sew that on at the bottom.

CHRISTMAS TREE
DECORATION

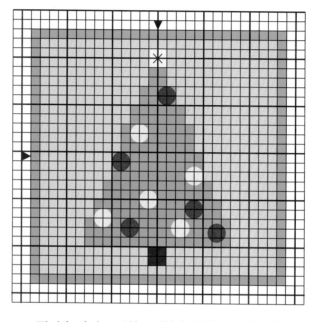

Finished size: 2½ × 2½ in (6.5 × 6.5 cm)

KEY

☐	**8114**
	9096
	8990
■	**9640**
○	**245** *French knot*
●	**901** *French knot*
×	**bead**

THIS IS A PERFECT DESIGN TO HANG ON A CHRISTMAS TREE. FOR A REALLY STUNNING DISPLAY, WORK SEVERAL OF THESE DESIGNS, CHANGING THE COLOURS SO THAT YOU USE A RANGE OF BRIGHT YELLOWS, REDS AND ORANGES AS BACKGROUND SHADES.

MATERIALS

- Tapestry wool: 1 skein each of 8990 and 9096; short lengths of 9640 and 8114
- Plastic canvas yarn: short lengths of 245 and 901
- 2 pieces of 12-hole interlock canvas, each 5 × 5 in (12.5 × 12.5 cm)
- 2 gold beads
- Polyester toy stuffing

1 Follow the chart to work the design, starting in the middle (indicated by the arrows on the edges). Use half cross stitch throughout. The colours on the chart and in the key correspond with the wool and yarn colours and numbers. Stitch two sides the same.

2 Add some French knots in bright colours. I have used plastic canvas yarn for these because it is thicker.

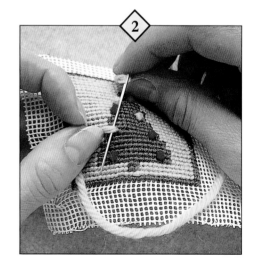

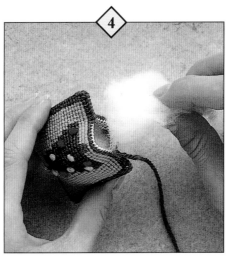

3 After stretching the embroidery, press it with a hot steam iron over a damp cloth, and trim back the canvas, cutting the corners at an angle. Stitch on the bead. Stitch the two sides together, leaving a gap for the stuffing.

4 Stuff with polyester toy stuffing.

5 Stitch the gap. Add a loop of yarn at the top, ends tied together in a bow.

S N O W M A N   C A R D

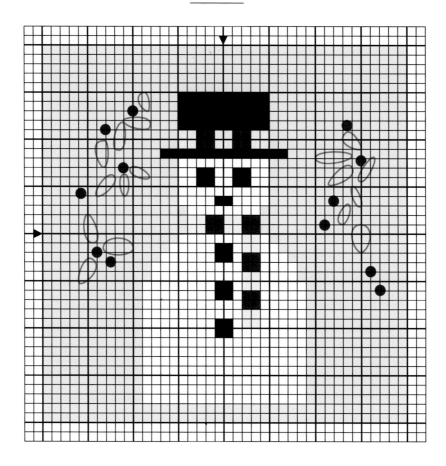

Finished size: 2½ in (6.5 cm) in diameter

KEY	
▢	1
▢	1212/94 *(mixed)*
▢	288
◼	46
●	46 *French knots*
◼	403
⬭	227 *chain stitch*

THIS DELIGHTFUL CARD CAN ALSO BE MADE INTO A FRAMED PICTURE TO GIVE A LONG-LASTING REMINDER OF CHRISTMAS. METALLIC THREAD IS USED IN THE BACKGROUND TO GIVE A SUBTLE SPARKLE, AND FRENCH KNOTS AND CHAIN STITCH ARE USED TO MAKE THE LEAVES AND BERRIES. GREETINGS CARDS FOR MOUNTING EMBROIDERY ARE AVAILABLE FROM NEEDLECRAFT AND HABERDASHERY SHOPS.

M A T E R I A L S

- Stranded cotton: 1 skein each of 1212 and 1; short lengths of 403, 288, 46 and 227
- Kreinik metallic thread: short lengths of 94
- 1 piece of 14-hole interlock canvas, 4 × 4 in (10 × 10 cm)
- Card with ready-cut mount
- Double-sided adhesive tape

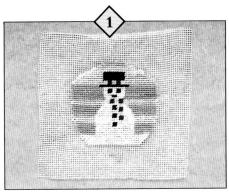

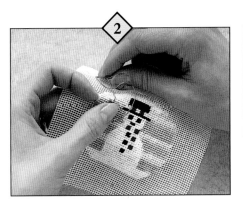

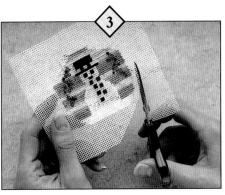

1 Follow the chart to work the design, starting in the middle (indicated by the arrows on the edges). Use half cross stitch throughout. The colours on the chart and in the key correspond with the stranded cotton and metallic thread colours and numbers.

2 After stitching the design, add the leaves in chain stitch and the red berries in French knots. You can stitch the snowman's mouth in cross stitch.

3 After stretching the embroidery, press it with a hot steam iron over a damp cloth, and trim back the canvas.

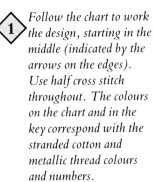

4 Add a piece of double-sided adhesive tape to the top and bottom of the embroidery and carefully position the card mount on top.

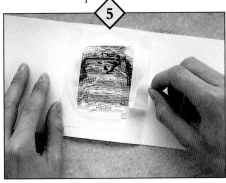

5 Secure the embroidery in position with more double-sided adhesive tape and close the left-hand mount to finish.

WINTER
HONEYSUCKLE
PINCUSHION

 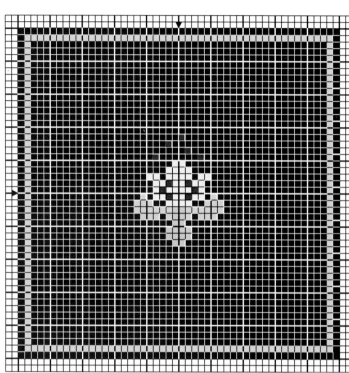

KEY	
	8016
	8136
	8392
	8442
	9100
	9600
	9800

Finished size: 4 × 4 in (10 × 10 cm)

A PINCUSHION IS ALWAYS USEFUL, BUT IF YOU ADD SOME SCENTED HERBS TO THE STUFFING YOU CAN MAKE A PRETTY POT POURRI SACHET. THIS DESIGN HAS A BLACK BACKGROUND, BUT YOU CAN USE A LIGHTER, CREAMY COLOUR INSTEAD IF YOU PREFER.

MATERIALS

- Tapestry wool: 1 skein of 8392; 3 skeins of 9800; short lengths of 8016, 8136, 8442, 9100 and 9600
- 2 pieces of 12-hole interlock canvas, each 7 × 7 in (17.5 × 17.5 cm)
- Polyester toy stuffing

1 *Follow the chart to work the design, starting in the middle (indicated by the arrows on the edges). Use half cross stitch throughout. The colours on the charts and in the key correspond with the wool colours and numbers.*

2 *After stretching the embroidery, press it with a hot steam iron over a damp cloth, and trim back the canvas, cutting the corners at an angle.*

3 *Stitch the two sides together, leaving a small gap for the stuffing.*

4 *Stuff the pincushion with polyester toy stuffing.*

5 *Stitch the gap.*